PRACTICAL READING STRATEGIES

PRACTICAL READING STRATEGIES

Engaging Activities for Secondary Students

Leon Furze

Published by Amba Press
Melbourne, Australia
www.ambapress.com.au

Editor – Rica Dearman
Cover Designer – Alissa Dinallo

Printed by IngramSpark

ISBN: 9781922607164 (pbk)
ISBN: 9781922607171 (ebk)

A catalogue record for this book is available from the National Library of Australia.

For Emily

ACKNOWLEDGEMENTS

Writing this book has given me the opportunity to pull together over a decade's worth of learning in the English classroom. First of all, I would like to thank my students. From my teacher training in the UK to my English and Literature classes in Australia, I could not have developed these skills without the constant support, feedback, challenge and energy of those I have taught. Similarly, I would like to thank my colleagues at Monivae College, Hamilton, who have been mentors, co-workers and guinea pigs as we have worked together to develop these strategies and activities.

I also wish to thank the amazing team at the Victorian Association for the Teaching of English. Without the guidance of the VATE community, this book would not exist. Through VATE conferences, workshops and professional learning, I have grown as an English teacher in ways I could not have imagined. Special thanks go to Mary Mason and Dr Amanda McGraw-Phleban, facilitators of the VATE Reading Community of Practice. Mary – your passion for shaking up the system of the English curriculum and putting students first will always colour my teaching.

Thanks to Alicia Cohen at Amba Press for reaching out to see whether I had a book in me, after reading a few of my English blog posts. There's a bit of a leap from a weekly blog to a full-blown book, but with your support and guidance, *Practical Reading Strategies* has come to life. Thanks also to Rica Dearman, who edited *PRS* with speed, precision and professionalism.

Finally, the biggest thanks go to my wife, Emily, and my children. Throughout all stages of my career, you have shown me support, generosity and love. Try as I might to be quiet when I sneak out to my desk in the morning to write, I'm sure I've woken you all up with the coffee machine more than once. Juggling writing, teaching and family can be tricky, but you have made it possible.

CONTENTS

INTRODUCTION

What is reading?

Before launching into a book of Reading Strategies, it pays to understand what reading actually *is*. Is reading picking up a text and following the words with your eyes? Is it understanding that text and knowing the content? Is it being able to see the content in your mind's eye? Or the ability to recount the information gleaned from the text? What about visual texts, such as pictures and movies – do we read them? And is listening to an audiobook reading with your ears, or a different process entirely?

The truth is, reading is an incredibly complex process and one that, for most people, is learned at an early stage of cognitive development. The complex processes involved in reading – such as phonemic and morphemic awareness, syntactic understanding and knowledge of the 'rules' language (Rayner & Reichle, 2010) – mean that when we ask the question 'what is reading?', we need to be prepared to go down the rabbit hole.

When I took on the role of Head of English in 2017, this question was high on our agenda. We joined the Victorian Association for the Teaching of English (VATE) in a community of practice research project in an effort to answer it. Rather than beginning with the question 'what is reading?', however, the Year 7 teachers – myself included – were instructed to ask the students 'how does reading make you feel?'

The connection with reading on an emotional as well as a logical level became one of the underpinning factors of the reading project. In response to that initial prompt, students drew illustrations of reading that ranged from magical book-filled worlds to shark-infested waters. The reason that reading prompts such a visceral reaction in some students – and some adults – is as complex as the definition itself. A web of situational, contextual factors impacts upon a person's individual experience of reading (Gee, 2004). Some of these factors include: early education; time spent reading at home in infancy; access to books; socioeconomic status; cognitive ability; level of technology use; and quality of instruction (Scholastic Corporation, 2021).

The further we probe the question, the deeper we descend into the complexities of a reader's context. And on a personal level, reading is also a unique and individual experience. Even among the teachers, we had broad-ranging definitions of what occurs behind our eyes when we read. For some, reading offers up a full sensory experience: moving pictures, sounds and smells, or memories associated with the words on the page. For others, the experience is more like a series of stills or black and white photographs. Some, such as those with aphantasia – the inability to create mental pictures – may be able to render only small portions of text at a time, if at all (Clemens, 2021).

So, in trying to answer the question 'what is reading?', we ultimately decided that attempting to define such a complex process, a process impacted by cultural, physical, mental and social factors, would be fruitless. None of the existing definitions of reading capture the entire picture, and rather than attempting to reduce or refine those definitions, we shifted our attention to focus on a different question: 'how can we teach reading?'

Overview of the Reading Strategies

Once we reframed the question, we found that the process became much more straightforward. To target and develop the many complex facets of reading, we began investigating methods of instruction that complemented different aspects. We returned to the VATE community of practice in 2019 with a suite of lessons and ideas that developed students' ability to read through close reading, explicit vocabulary and grammar instruction, contextual and social activities, dramatic activities and more. Alongside VATE, we formed our own six Reading Strategies:

1. Making Connections
2. Visualising
3. Questioning
4. Inferring
5. Summarising
6. Synthesising

The six Reading Strategies gave us a framework around which to develop our whole-school approach to reading: a system. It allowed us to investigate how a given activity might encourage a student to *connect* with the text on a personal, contextual level, and then lead naturally on to another, which encourages them to *question* for themselves aspects of the text. The *inferring* strategy highlighted a major gap in our existing system: we had spent a lot of time teaching students *what* to think about text, but not *how* to think.

The Reading Strategies are not hierarchical, but there is logic to the order. Most teachers will be familiar with Bloom's taxonomy. Sometimes, in teacher education, Bloom's taxonomy is held up as a fixed and linear approach to cognition. Subsequent research into how we think has challenged that notion. The excellent work from Project Zero at Harvard University, which resulted in the Visible Thinking Routines, suggests that at any given time we might range across multiple categories (Morrison, Ritchhart & Church, 2013).

We tend to think of the Reading Strategies as the latter, moving between Strategies and activities as needed rather than progressing through them in a linear fashion. It is useful, however, to arrange them in a hierarchy when first using them.

Comparison of the Reading Strategies to Bloom's taxonomy

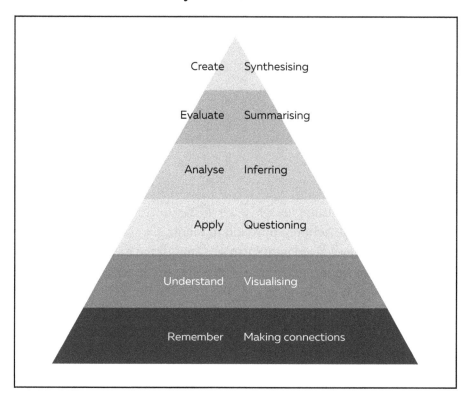

This book is less concerned with the theory of how we developed the Reading Strategies, and more with putting practical activities into the hands of teachers. In our experience, the best way to find out what works for your students is to step into the classroom and start teaching.

How to use this book

Each of the six Strategies in this book is demonstrated with four unique activities. These are by no means the *only* way to explore each Strategy, but they will give teachers a good idea of the kinds of skills used in each area. Of course, the Strategies are just a convenient way of organising very complex skill sets, so an activity that is found in the chapter on Making Connections could very well be used as a Questioning activity with a little manipulation. There is more on this in part two, in the chapter on Combining Strategies.

Each Strategy chapter follows the same format:

Four activities, split into:
- Instructions for teachers
- Instructions for students
- Example
- Reflect
- Extend

Instructions for teachers

In the instructions for teachers you will find an overview of the resources (physical or digital) required to complete the activity, plus a step-by-step process including anything required before the lesson to set up. The instructions for teachers are designed to be as comprehensive as possible, and sometimes include scripts for discussing the activity with students.

Instructions for students

The instructions for students are a condensed version of the instructions for teachers. They are deliberately concise so that they can be easily copied and shared with students. These instructions do not need to be handed out to students for every activity; sometimes the teacher's verbal instructions will suffice, and sometimes the framework or graphic organiser provided for the activity is self-explanatory.

Example

In the example section you will find a completed version of the task. Many of these are reproduced with permission from actual students. Some are an amalgam of various student responses that I have pulled together as an example. In all cases, the activities have been completed by real students and trialled and tweaked on more than one occasion. In some instances (like the Text File in the Synthesising chapter), a complete example would be too large to include here and so extracts are used to demonstrate the key aspects of the activity. Blank templates within the examples are available in the Appendix and for download.

Reflect

The reflection section of each activity is an important opportunity to think about the impact of the activity with *your* students. In some cases, it would be good to review the reflection prompts *before* completing the activity. For example, there are moments when you might wish to discuss the activity with your team and make some changes for your particular cohort of students beforehand. In other instances, the reflect questions encourage you to review how the activity went, and what could be done differently next time.

Extend

Each activity concludes with suggestions for how to extend. These could be opportunities for highly able students to push themselves further, or suggestions for follow-up activities. In some cases, the extend section may lead towards a summative task such as an essay or creative piece.

Part two of the book provides a bigger-picture overview of how the Strategies can be used, firstly within an English classroom, then an English faculty, and then at a whole-school level to support literacy across various disciplines. In part two you will find examples of individual units of work and whole-unit sequences, as well as examples of various activities from each Strategy with resources from different faculties. Again, these are not intended to be *the only* ways to use the Strategies in other disciplines; like part one, the examples and reflections are intended as conversation starters.

PART 1

CHAPTER 1

STRATEGY 1: MAKING CONNECTIONS

An important first step in introducing a new text to students is to leverage the "resources that [students] bring" to the classroom (Billman & Pearson, 2013). By activating the prior knowledge of students – their context, history, prior readings and experiences – we can shortcut some of the process of explaining or explicitly teaching new ideas.

Keene and Zimmerman (1997) refer to students' ability to make connections in three ways:

Text-to-self

Good readers constantly make internal references to their own lived experiences and the text in front of them. The more of themselves a reader sees in a text, the easier it will be to decode. Young adult fiction, for example, is not just popular because it is 'more simplistic' than the classics or more complex prose. Students can more often see themselves in a text written for their age group and can more easily relate to the characters, situations and settings. The cognitive load of processing the text is reduced when aspects of the text mirror the reader's own lived experience.

Text-to-text

Part of any reader's experience is also formed by other texts they have encountered. This may include other forms of media such as television, film and digital. A student with a wide repertoire of prior reading will find it much easier to access new texts that are related to things they have seen before. But text-to-text connections are not just the privilege of strong readers: leveraging *intertextual* knowledge can be done deliberately in the classroom by preparing reading material *around* a core text, engineering connections for students who may not have encountered them before (see Activity 3: Context Walk).

Text-to-world

The bigger-picture connections of text-to-world include a reader's understanding of the contexts in which texts are written, as well as the global context in which they live. Understanding major historical events – for example, the world wars, 9/11, colonisation and the displacement of indigenous peoples – provides another connection, which reduces the cognitive load of reading new texts.

James Gee (2004) discusses that, "All words take on nuanced meanings in context and they can take on new meanings in new contexts." These 'situated meanings' of words are highly dependent on a student's ability to make connections – to themselves, other texts and the world around them.

The following activities target all three of Keene and Zimmerman's connections, either focusing on them individually, or taking them as a group. The activities use annotation, discussion and reflection to draw connections to the core text. Beginning with the simplest – but possibly most versatile – of the activities, the Text Walk, students will explicitly identify links to extracts of a central text. This idea is then expanded upon in a contextualising activity, and further developed through coding and finally mapping. Like the Strategies themselves, the four activities are not necessarily hierarchical, but there is a logic to completing them in order when first introducing students to the techniques involved.

Before completing any of these activities, make sure that students are familiar with Keene and Zimmerman's three types of connection. For example, discuss each of the types using the text currently being studied, modelling your own responses as follows:

Example

Text: *The Hunger Games* by Suzanne Collins

Text-to-self

Texts can remind us of events from our own lives. I've never been part of a lottery that throws me into a fight to the death like Katniss Everdeen, but I have been responsible for looking after a younger sibling, and I know what responsibility feels like. I also learned to shoot a bow and arrow at school, and I've been on wilderness camps where we've had to use survival skills.

Text-to-text

Sometimes when we are reading new texts, we are reminded of texts we have seen and read before. Texts can include other books, films, television, fiction and nonfiction. For example, when I'm reading *The Hunger Games*, I'm reminded of other dystopian books I've read, such as the *Divergent* series and Lois Lowry's *The Giver*. It also reminds me of television shows like the Netflix series *Shadow and Bone* and *The 100*.

Text-to-world

Stories are based on real-world events, even fictional narratives like *The Hunger Games*. Some parts of the novel remind me of the real world, like the class divides between the different districts, the corruption of the people in charge and how the games is almost like a microcosm (a miniature version) of a bigger conflict like war.

ACTIVITY 1: CONNECTIONS CODING

Coding is the use of symbols and systems when annotating a text. This can be done with visual symbols, like ! for important points and ? for questions, or by colour coding. In this activity, students annotate a text looking for the three types of connection:

- Text-to-self: Links to the reader's own life and experience.
- Text-to-text: Intertextual links to other texts the reader has experienced, including visual texts.
- Text-to-world: Links to the wider world, including issues currently in the media.

This activity should be completed by students as individuals, but the skills learned can be transferred into the following group activities.

Instructions for teachers

☑ An extract from the central text on paper, or on a digital document
☑ Highlighters and pens/pencils or digital-annotation tools

1. Before beginning this activity, ensure students are familiar with the three types of connection. See the introduction of this chapter for advice.
2. Select a short passage for annotation. The length and complexity of the passage should be determined by the capability of the students – you may choose to vary the passages to differentiate for individual students.
3. Choose either colour coding or symbol coding, for example:
   a. Text-to-self or TTS
   b. Text-to-text or TTT
   c. Text-to-world or TTW

4. Instruct students to read and annotate the extract for the three connections. As well as colour/symbol coding, students should make brief margin notes to explain the connection.
5. Discuss connections in groups or as a class.

Instructions for students

Read the text carefully. As you read, make notes on any of the following connections:

◆ Text-to-self: Links to the reader's own life and experience.
◆ Text-to-text: Intertextual links to other texts the reader has experienced, including visual texts.
◆ Text-to-world: Links to the wider world, including issues currently in the media.

Use symbols (TTS, TTT, TTW) or colours to annotate the text. Make sure you also add brief notes to explain.

Example

In this example the student has found one of each kind of connection to an extract from *Little Women*. This helps the student to not only connect with the details on a personal level (like the memories of their own Christmases), but also to connect vocabulary from other lessons (for example, the word 'pilgrim' from Humanities or Religion).

From *Little Women* by Louisa May Alcott

TTW
Northern
Hemisphere
Xmas is
cold!

Jo was the first to wake in the gray dawn of Christmas morning. No stockings hung at the fireplace, and for a moment she felt as much disappointed as she did long ago, when her little sock fell down because it was crammed so full of goodies. Then she remembered her mother's promise and, slipping her hand under her pillow, drew out a little crimson-covered book. She knew it very well, for it was that beautiful old story of the best life ever lived, and Jo felt that it was a true guidebook for any pilgrim going on a long journey. She woke Meg with a "Merry Christmas," and bade her see what was under her pillow. A green-covered book appeared, with the same picture inside, and a few words written by their mother, which made their one present very precious in their eyes. Presently Beth and Amy woke to rummage and find their little books also, one dove-colored, the other blue, and all sat looking at and talking about them, while the east grew rosy with the coming day.

TTS
Remember
being
disappointed
when we got
'too old' for
stockings

TTT
Learned about
pilgrimages in
hums/RE

Reflect

I've had some success with using an 'off-the-shelf' set of codes, such as the extensive system used in Judith C Hochman and Natalie Wexler's 2017 book *The Writing Revolution*, but in the end, I always come back to a sort of hybrid of my suggestions and the students' own systems. I find that once a coding system reaches the point where it must be turned into a cut-and-paste key – stick this in the front of your exercise books – it's gone too far. Your codes and symbols should be few and memorable, otherwise they'll never get used. Similarly, if students have some autonomy over what symbols and systems they use, they're much more likely to use them.

- TTS, TTT and TTW work for this exercise. What other 'codes' could students use to annotate text?
- Where do you draw the line with symbols and codes for annotation? Do you subscribe to the Harvard advice of "throw away your highlighter", using only pen or pencils for margin notes, or will you use a colour-coding system?
- What interesting and unique forms of annotation have you come across from your own students? Dog-earing pages, torn-up bookmarks, sticky notes – whatever works for them should be encouraged.

Extend

Coding activities are a useful starting point for deeper discussions and extended written tasks. The individual students' annotations from this activity could be used for:

- Group discussions based on the three connection types
- A sentence or paragraph based on one or more of the connection types
- A whole-class discussion on the similarities and differences between readers' annotations

ACTIVITY 2: CONNECTIONS TEXT WALK

The Text Walk – sometimes called a Chalk Talk – is an essential activity that can be used across the Reading Strategies. Here, it is used to highlight connections between the student and the text(s) being studied.

A Text Walk can be completed with extracts from a single text or multiple. Activity 3, the Context Walk, builds on this idea and uses multimodal texts.

Instructions for teachers

☑ Five to eight extracts from the central text on A3 paper, or extracts on a digital shared document (one extract per page)
☑ Highlighters and pens/pencils or digital-annotation tools

1. To set up, select extracts from the text(s) you are studying. The activity can be completed physically with extracts at the centre of A3 sheets, or digitally using a shared document. Place one extract/text at the centre of each page, for up to eight pages.
2. Begin this activity by discussing the three different types of connection: text-to-self, text-to-text and text-to-world. If you are running a Text Walk for the first time, you may wish to focus on just one.
3. Place the extracts around the room and assign students to groups of three or four. Station each group at an extract.
4. Students have a set amount of time at each extract. I'd recommend between 30 seconds and three minutes, depending on the length and complexity of the extracts. During this time, the students should read, discuss and annotate. They should annotate TTS, TTT or TTW connections.

5. After the time limit, the group should move on to the next extract. Students may respond to other groups' notes in their annotations.
6. Continue until each group has had an opportunity to annotate each extract.
7. After the activity, scan, photograph or otherwise display the annotated extracts for whole-class discussion. What were identified as the key parts of the extracts? What connections did the students highlight?

Instructions for students

Your group will have a set time to spend on each extract. Read and discuss the extract, and then make notes on any connections you can make:

- Text-to-self
- Text-to-text
- Text-to-world

As you move around, you may add notes to what other groups have written.

Example

From *A Christmas Carol* by Charles Dickens

TTT
COUNTING
HOUSES IN
OTHER
  DICKENS
    BOOKS

TTS
We get fog
like this
in
winter

TTS
REMINDS ME
OF SMOG WHEN
I VISITED BEIJING

Once upon a time—of all the good days in the year, on Christmas Eve—old Scrooge sat busy in his counting-house. It was cold, bleak, biting weather: foggy withal: and he could hear the people in the court outside, go wheezing up and down, beating their hands upon their breasts, and stamping their feet upon the pavement stones to warm them. The city clocks had only just gone three, but it was quite dark already—it had not been light all day—and candles were flaring in the windows of the neighbouring offices, like ruddy smears upon the palpable brown air. The fog came pouring in at every chink and keyhole, and was so dense without, that although the court was of the narrowest, the houses opposite were mere phantoms. To see the dingy cloud come drooping down, obscuring everything, one might have thought that Nature lived hard by, and was brewing on a large scale.

TTW
why is it
cold at
Christmas?
tts reminds me
of London
    IT-S
    IN
    ENGLAND!
TTW
Dark at
three?!

TTS
I can picture
dingy days like
this

TTW
Must be a
long time
ago before
cars

tts
we have
decorations
like
these

Meanwhile the fog and darkness thickened so, that people ran about with flaring links, proffering their services to go before horses in carriages, and conduct them on their way. The ancient tower of a church, whose gruff old bell was always peeping slily down at Scrooge out of a Gothic window in the wall, became invisible, and struck the hours and quarters in the clouds, with tremulous vibrations afterwards as if its teeth were chattering in its frozen head up there. The cold became intense. In the main street, at the corner of the court, some labourers were repairing the gas-pipes, and had lighted a great fire in a brazier, round which a party of ragged men and boys were gathered: warming their hands and winking their eyes before the blaze in rapture. The water-plug being left in solitude, its overflowings sullenly congealed, and turned to misanthropic ice. The brightness of the shops where holly sprigs and berries crackled in the lamp heat of the windows, made pale faces ruddy as they passed.

TTT
LIKE
FRANKENSTEIN
AND DRACULA

TTW REMINDS
ME OF INDUSTRIAL
REVOLUTION FROM
HISTORY

Reflect

This is one of my most-used activities, with any text and at any point during study: beginning, middle or end. It encourages discussion, allows every student to have a voice in the conversation and, importantly, removes the teacher from the equation, which can often be a good thing. Ultimately, students will need to form their own meaning from texts and encouraging them to make connections is a great place to start. The first few times you run this activity you'll likely have to contend with students writing (or drawing) inappropriate things on the pages. Assign your students unique colours or make a digital text walk with students signed into their accounts, if you like. I've only had to resort to such authoritarian measures a couple of times, most notably with a class of Year 8s who favoured questionable drawings over written notes. They got over it eventually, and the Text Walk was established as a classroom routine. Before or after trying this activity, reflect on the following:

- What does 'removing the teacher from the equation' achieve in the Text Walk activity?
- Students have a vast range of different experiences. Some will have a lot of context around your texts, others very little. What issues does this present, and what can the teacher do about those issues?
- What are the benefits of conducting the Text Walk as a group versus an individual activity?

Extend

The Text Walk can be used in a variety of situations and is a useful activity for any of the Strategies. As you read on, consider how the Text Walk can be used to develop questions, visualise, build inferences, summarise and synthesise, for example:

- Prompting students to expand their connections with guided questions like, "Given the similarity to a real-life event, how would you have acted in the character's situation?"
- Asking students to annotate only with questions they have about the meaning of the extracts
- Asking students to annotate for sensory or figurative language
- Asking students to annotate for inferences and observations

ACTIVITY 3:
CONTEXT WALK

This is a variation on the standard Text Walk, which shortcuts the need for some of the 'situated meaning' required to understand complex texts. Rather than spend a long time contextualising a text – for example, spending lengthy research tasks diving into World War II – the Context Walk provides a snapshot of related texts around a genre, historical event or issue relevant to the central text.

Instructions for teachers

☑ Five to eight extracts from contextualising resources on A3 paper, or extracts on a digital shared document (one extract per page). Aim for a multimodal selection including nonfiction, fiction, photographs and artwork (and videos with a digital Context Walk)

☑ Highlighters and pens/pencils or digital-annotation tools

1. Set up this activity in the same way as the Text Walk. Instead of extracts from the central text(s), use multimodal extracts – including images, film stills, fiction and nonfiction – that encircle the genre, events or issues of the central text.

2. Conduct the Text Walk in the same way as Activity 1. Instead of annotating for TTS, TTT and TTW connections, the students should take notes on the common features and connections between the extracts.

3. After the activity, scan, photograph or otherwise display the annotated extracts for whole-class discussion. What were identified as the key parts of the extracts? What connections did the students highlight?

Instructions for students

Your group will have a set time to spend on each extract. Read and discuss the extract, and then make notes on any connections you can make between the extracts. Focus on:

- Key ideas, issues and themes
- The language used
- Visual techniques

As you move around, you may add notes to what other groups have written.

Example

The following are examples of contextualising materials for a study on any war literature, for example, Markus Zusak's *The Book Thief* or Michael Morpurgo's *Private Peaceful*. Note how the students have drawn heavily on their own experiences (seeing ANZAC parades, learning about war in History, even relating the descriptions to recent events during the pandemic).

A close-up of the Holocaust memorial in Berlin

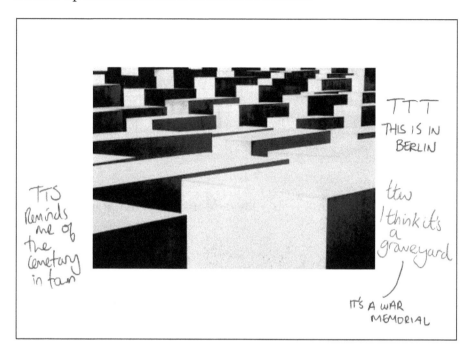

The *Phantom Horseman* (1870–93) by Sir John Gilbert

From *History of the World War* by Francis A March and Richard J Beamish

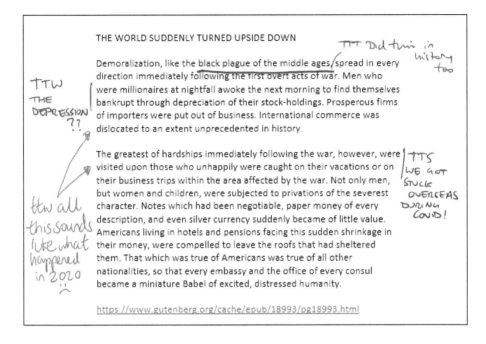

THE WORLD SUDDENLY TURNED UPSIDE DOWN

Demoralization, like the black plague of the middle ages, spread in every direction immediately following the first overt acts of war. Men who were millionaires at nightfall awoke the next morning to find themselves bankrupt through depreciation of their stock-holdings. Prosperous firms of importers were put out of business. International commerce was dislocated to an extent unprecedented in history.

The greatest of hardships immediately following the war, however, were visited upon those who unhappily were caught on their vacations or on their business trips within the area affected by the war. Not only men, but women and children, were subjected to privations of the severest character. Notes which had been negotiable, paper money of every description, and even silver currency suddenly became of little value. Americans living in hotels and pensions facing this sudden shrinkage in their money, were compelled to leave the roofs that had sheltered them. That which was true of Americans was true of all other nationalities, so that every embassy and the office of every consul became a miniature Babel of excited, distressed humanity.

https://www.gutenberg.org/cache/epub/18993/pg18993.html

Handwritten annotations:
- TTT Did this in history too
- TTW THE DEPRESSION ??
- ttw all this sounds like what happened in 2020
- TTS WE GOT STUCK OVERSEAS DURING COVID!

From *Anthem for Doomed Youth* by Wilfred Owen

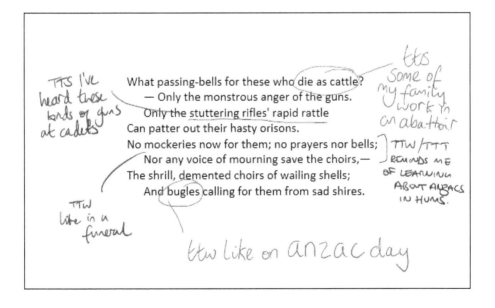

What passing-bells for these who die as cattle?
— Only the monstrous anger of the guns.
Only the stuttering rifles' rapid rattle
Can patter out their hasty orisons.
No mockeries now for them; no prayers nor bells;
Nor any voice of mourning save the choirs,—
The shrill, demented choirs of wailing shells;
And bugles calling for them from sad shires.

Handwritten annotations:
- TTS I've heard these kinds of guns at cadets
- tts Some of my family work in an abattoir
- TTW/TTT REMINDS ME OF LEARNING ABOUT ANZACS IN HUMS.
- TTW like in a funeral
- ttw like on ANZAC day

Reflect

Many English teachers have Humanities as a second method, and even for those of us who do not, we can be tempted to spend a great deal of time contextualising texts. I once ended up down the rabbit hole discussing World War I for a whole week before I realised that they'd already heard most of it in History. Nobody interrupted me while I grandstanded on the context surrounding Wilfred Owen's poems, but I suspect that we would have been better off spending that week looking at the poems themselves. Consider:

- What are the benefits of not providing much context, and letting the text speak for itself?
- How else could you provide brief 'bursts' of context to support students who may lack a contextual understanding of their own?
- Is there anything you can do to capitalise on context from other subject areas?

Extend

Like the regular Text Walk, the Context Walk can be used across the Reading Strategies. See Activity 1 for some ideas of how to adapt for questioning, inferring and so on. Additionally:

- Create a digital Context Walk of short video clips.
- Flip the task so that groups of students are responsible for creating the materials for the Context Walk.
- Remove the context from the English classroom entirely, and suggest to your colleagues in the Humanities class that they could use a Context Walk to give you a helping hand (and a couple of extra lessons).

ACTIVITY 4: CONNECTIONS MAP

Mapping activities can be used across a range of Strategies and work very well for drawing connections. You'll find other examples of mapping activities in both the Summarising and Synthesising chapters. Using physical space to indicate the strength of connections is also a great way of reinforcing knowledge and ideas.

In a Connections Map activity (also known as a 'concept map'), the students might focus on one of the three types of connections, or all of them.

Instructions for teachers

☑ Space to create the concept map, such as A3 paper, butcher's paper, a whiteboard (or whiteboard table) or a digital space such as Google Jamboard, Padlet and so on

1. This activity is best conducted at the end of studying a text or passage. It is also a good option as a follow-up for any of the previous connections activities to consolidate the knowledge.
2. Discuss the key connections uncovered in the study of a text. This might include a summary of the previous activities in text-to-self, text-to-text or text-to-world connections.
3. Highlight the main connections and use these as the key concepts for a concept map. At its simplest level, a concept map is a brainstorm of ideas coming from a central point, in this case, connections.
4. For more complex maps, students could indicate the strength of a connection by its size, its proximity to other connections or by annotating the lines/arrows that link connections together.

Instructions for students

Think about all the connections you have made with the text. These might be:

◆ Text-to-self: Links to your own life
◆ Text-to-text: Links to other texts you've read and seen
◆ Text-to-world: Links to the wider world

Map out the connections, drawing links between your ideas. You might choose to highlight the importance of some connections by making them bigger or clustering together similar ideas.

Example

In this example, students have mapped text-to-text connections between Anna Funder's *Stasiland* and Kazuo Ishiguro's *Never Let Me Go*. Key concepts that link the texts (the darker shade of grey) are surrounded by supporting ideas (the lighter shade of grey). Some of the ideas have been further connected by lines. The students have also used the size and proximity of the sticky notes to indicate importance and connection.

Example of text-to-text Connections Map for *Stasiland* and *Never Let Me Go*

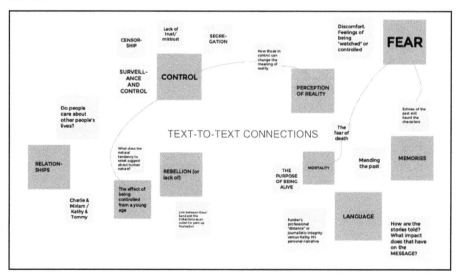

Reflect

This example came from a Year 12 class on *Stasiland* and *Never Let Me Go*. While the comparative writing task is on its way out of the curriculum in Victoria, the skills of text-to-text comparison cannot be understated. I used to teach a Year 10 unit on Victorian Gothic literature, one of my personal favourites. One year, we had the idea to prepare students over the holidays by giving them a reading list of both Victorian and contemporary Gothic and horror novels, ranging from classics like *Frankenstein* to modern fiction for children, like the *A Series of Unfortunate Events* books. The students who made the effort over summer to attempt even one or two of the suggested books arrived with much more readiness to tackle the genre. Before trying this activity, think about the following:

♦ Can you create your own concept map of TTT connections for the next book you're going to teach? What other texts have you come across that might support the central text? Can you make a reading list for students that might help them out?

♦ If it's unlikely that your students will engage with even more reading, is there a way you can do something similar for TTS or TTW connections? A 'reading list' of personal experiences might sound bizarre, but a few prompts like 'have you ever been frightened?' or 'have you ever been somewhere that – for no particular reason – creeped you out?' might pave the way for a Gothic unit.

Extend

Concept maps are extremely versatile. Take this idea and extend it with some of the following suggestions:

♦ Concept maps of any kind work well as both individual and group activities. Take individual students' maps and combine them in groups to make more comprehensive maps, which reflect the class understanding of the text.

- Because mapping is a metacognitive process, it is also a useful activity to use prior to extended written tasks.
- Create separate maps for the three areas of connection: self, text and world. Combine them at the end for a hugely useful resource that students can use as they continue to study the text.

CHAPTER 2

STRATEGY 2: VISUALISING

When I use the word 'visualising', I speak in the sense of 'forming a mental picture'. For me, this includes a full sensory experience. When I read, I experience a text in full technicolour and with sounds, smells and textures. Reading isn't the same for everyone, however, and these activities exist to encourage even struggling readers to build a mental picture of a text, drawing on as much sensory information as possible.

It's helpful to keep all five senses – plus a bonus one – front of mind when conducting these activities. It can be easy enough to get a student to draw a scene from a text, relying purely on visual information. But bringing in smells, sounds, textures and tastes can be much more difficult. The more sensory detail you can associate with a text, however, the easier it is for a student to process the content in their working memory (Quak, London & Talsma, 2015).

Sight

This is the easiest to access of the senses for most students. Studies even suggest that people with congenital blindness use their visual cortex for processing sensory information, meaning that multimodal information – such as touch or 'haptic' information – can be used to form mental pictures (Gilbert, Reiner & Nakhleh, 2008). Students will be familiar with common visualising activities such as storyboards and illustrations that rely on a predominantly visual understanding of text.

Sound

Even though the popular 'learning styles' understanding of visual-auditory-kinaesthetic learners has been generally debunked, there is truth in the understanding that some students respond better to verbal instructions than written instructions, while others find a mixture of both useful (Khazan, 2021). Activities that engage the sense of sound, like Activity 2: Soundscapes, encourage students to build a mental picture beyond just the visual.

Smell

Smells are known to trigger evocative and sometimes fully sensory memories, partly because of how smells seem to totally bypass the 'relay station' of the brain, the thalamus (Hamer, 2021). I haven't had an English lesson where I've been able to conjure up the smells of Dickens' London – nor would I want to – but the sense of smell can play an important role in evoking strong mental images across a range of disciplines. Think of the smell of sulphur, a freshly mown wicket or a vanilla pod.

Touch

As mentioned above, touch can be an ideal substitute for sight. The fingertips are so sensitive that we can register touch on the scale of a single fingerprint ridge (Bowler, 2021), and touch can aid or even supplant the formation of a visual image. Activities using objects with different textures, scraps of material representing characters or the various different textures of materials from a story's setting all provide an opportunity to engage this sense.

Taste

This is another sense that's possibly more difficult to evoke in some classes than others, but nonetheless it's a powerful one. A food technology class might be an obvious place for taste, and a science experiment is definitely *not* the right fit. But think about bringing in food – allergies and dietary requirements permitting – when exploring different places and cultures in English.

To the standard five I'll add one more sense, and it has nothing to do with reading minds or moving furniture around. It is the sense through which we understand the people around us, and which allows us to visualise not just a situation, but how a person thinks and feels.

Bonus sense: Empathy

Empathy is feeling *with* someone as opposed to feeling *for* (sympathy). In order to empathise, students must be able to also visualise, to imagine themselves in the other person's position, and to build a mental picture of their situation. I include empathy in the Visualising Strategy because of the importance of being able to visualise a character in a text, or a famous figure from a biography, or what it feels like to win an Olympic medal. To do all these things, a student must imagine what it is like to see, hear, smell, touch and taste the world in the same way as the people they read about.

ACTIVITY 1: SENSORY SCENES

As discussed in the introduction to this chapter, students should not be limited to just sight when they are Visualising texts. This activity encourages them to think about all of the sensory information that can be found in a scene.

Instructions for teachers

- ☑ A suitable text/extract with enough sensory detail for students to be able to find or infer information for all five of the senses
- ☑ A copy of the Sensory Scenes graphic organiser (see Appendix 1)
- ☑ Optional: Physical objects that represent textures for the 'touch' sense

1. Begin by studying the extract. For students who have not attempted this activity before, it may be useful to model annotating the extract to identify sensory information. Where explicit sensory detail cannot be found in the text, model how to *infer* the details (for example, 'what kind of sounds would you hear in this place?').
2. Allow students time to annotate the text.
3. Instruct students to complete the Sensory Scenes graphic organiser. Begin with the drawing (visual) at the centre of the organiser, and then complete the remaining sections.
4. Optional: If there is the opportunity for students to work on the graphic organiser at home, they could also include a small sample of material for the touch sense, for example, a scrap of fabric, material like sandpaper or aluminium foil, and so on.
5. Discuss the students' different interpretations of the scene as a class.

Instructions for students

Read the extract and annotate, looking for any sensory details such as sights, sounds, smells, tastes and textures.

Complete the Sensory Scenes graphic organiser. Begin by drawing the visuals from the scene in the central box, and then write notes in the remaining four.

Optional: Find a material to attach to the graphic organiser for the touch sense.

Example

Annotated extract from *The Yellow Wallpaper* by Charlotte Perkins Gilman

Sound - big/airy - maybe echoes

"Your exercise depends on your strength, my dear," said he, "and your food somewhat on your appetite; but air you can absorb all the time." So we took the nursery, at the top of the house.

It is a big, airy room, the whole floor nearly, with windows that look all ways, and air and sunshine galore. It was nursery first and then playground and gymnasium, I should judge; for the windows are barred for little children, and there are rings and things in the walls.

The paint and paper look as if a boys' school had used it. It is stripped off—the paper—in great patches all around the head of my bed, about as far as I can reach, and in a great place on the other side of

Smells - fresh air, outside

Smells - maybe old smells that linger from when children used the nursery

the room low down. I never saw a worse paper in my life. ←

Sight - the wallpaper v important, lots of description.

One of those sprawling flamboyant patterns committing every artistic sin.

It is dull enough to confuse the eye in following, pronounced enough to constantly irritate, and provoke study, and when you follow the lame, uncertain curves for a little distance they suddenly commit suicide—plunge off at outrageous angles, destroy themselves in unheard-of contradictions.

The color is repellant, almost revolting; a smouldering, unclean yellow, strangely faded by the slow-turning sunlight.

It is a dull yet lurid orange in some places, a sickly sulphur tint in others.

Sight - more description of the <u>yellow</u> wallpaper

No wonder the children hated it! I should hate it myself if I had to live in this room long.

Sensory Scenes

Name:

Text/extract:

Sounds: Describe the sounds	Smells: Describe the smells

Sight: Draw a picture of the scene

Taste: Describe the taste	Textures: Describe the textures or attach a material

Sensory Scenes

Name: Janey Jones

Text/extract: The Yellow Wallpaper – Charlotte Perkins Gilman

Sounds: Describe the sounds	Smells: Describe the smells
Echoes of footsteps. Noises of children (in the past). Conversation between John and the narrator.	Fresh air and outdoors smells through the window (cut grass). Lingering smells of children. Stale smell from the wallpaper.

Sight: Draw a picture of the scene

Taste: Describe the taste	Textures: Describe the textures or attach a material
Taste of the fresh air coming through the window.	

Reflect

Encouraging students to think beyond just a visual representation of the scene can be more engaging and can lead to some very different interpretations of the same scene. While the student in the example has identified the 'lingering smells' of the children who used the nursery in the past, another might focus more on the scents drifting in through the window or the texture of the bed rather than the peeling wallpaper. Every different interpretation can lead to a rich discussion with students about why they formed that impression, going back to their initial annotations.

In a story like *The Yellow Wallpaper*, which is an early feminist horror story, the sensory detail plays an incredibly important role. However, even in texts that are much sparser in sensory detail, an activity like this can be used to encourage students to dig in and make their own inferences.

- What texts have you read, taught or studied are particularly elegant in their sensory descriptions?
- What about texts that are deliberately lacking in sensory detail – how would that have an impact on this activity?
- The introduction to this chapter also mentions the 'sense' of *empathy*. Is there a place for empathy in this kind of scene analysis?

Extend

Building up a bank of detail on sensory information in a text can be useful for both analysis and creative writing. To extend this task, consider:

- Having students write a response to a prompt like: How does <author> use sensory detail to create <atmosphere, tension, a sense of time and place...>?
- Choosing one or more of the senses as a creative writing prompt, for example: Take the detail you have written for <sight, smell, sound, touch, taste> and write a new scene using that same detail
- Connect this activity to another in this chapter, such as building a Soundscape (Activity 2) based on the annotations and graphic organiser.

ACTIVITY 2: SOUNDSCAPES

Soundscapes are an aural landscape of a scene or a moment in the text, developed by the students. Getting students to use details from the text and their own imaginations is a great way of extending a visualisation beyond just sight and is an engaging and fun lesson.

Before beginning this activity, you may wish to conduct a quick survey of the students to see that they have the technology and the skills to complete the task. You'll be surprised how many will have used software like GarageBand in primary school and junior secondary, for example, in making podcasts. Never assume, however, that everyone in the class has access to the same quality of devices, or a stable internet connection at home. If that is the case, you can find ways to make this activity more accessible, for example, by downloading a range of stock audio clips yourself and having them available in a shared drive or on a USB drive.

Instructions for teachers

- ☑ A library of sounds, such as freesound.org (free, requires registration for some downloads). You could also create your own library before the lesson to reduce potential technology issues and also reduce the time students spend searching for materials
- ☑ Sound-editing software. GarageBand (MacOS, iOS) and Audacity (MacOS, Windows) are both good, free options that do not have too much of a steep learning curve
- ☑ A text with a scene or scenes suitable for developing a soundscape

1. Select the text for study and ensure students have read it either as a group or individually.

2. Annotate the text, identifying possible sources of sound in the background or setting, including direct quotes and implied sounds from the description.
3. Optional: As a class, discuss and brainstorm what other sources of sound might be found in the text. For example, discuss whether students have ever been somewhere similar to the setting of the text, and what they may have heard there.
4. Direct students to a sound library such as freesound.org or one you have prepared. From the library, students should select a range of sounds that may be found in the text.
5. Ask students to import the sounds into the editing software. Students can then layer up the different sounds. Students with more technical abilities may also be able to adjust the volume, fading and panning of sounds (the movement of the sound from the left speaker to the right or vice versa). See the example for more on this.
6. Ask each student to finish with a brief written explanation.
7. In groups or as a class, play the sounds back and compare different students' interpretations of the scene.

Instructions for students

Annotate the text, looking for anything that suggests sounds in the scene.

Think about what other sounds you might hear in this scene. Add those ideas to your annotations.

Browse the sound library and find some suitable sounds. Using editing software (for example, GarageBand or Audacity), layer up the sounds to create your soundscape.

Write a brief written explanation of your choices.

Example

From *Great Expectations* by Charles Dickens

When I told the clerk that I would take a turn in the air while I waited, he advised me to go round the corner and I should come into Smithfield. So I came into Smithfield; and the shameful place, being all asmear with filth and fat and blood and foam, seemed to stick to me. So, I rubbed it off with all possible speed by turning into a street where I saw the great black dome of Saint Paul's bulging at me from behind a grim stone building which a bystander said was Newgate Prison. Following the wall of the jail, I found the roadway covered with straw to deaden the noise of passing vehicles; and from this, and from the quantity of people standing about smelling strongly of spirits and beer, I inferred that the trials were on.

While I looked about me here, an exceedingly dirty and partially drunk minister of justice asked me if I would like to step in and hear a trial or so: informing me that he could give me a front place for half a crown, whence I should command a full view of the Lord Chief Justice in his wig and robes,—mentioning that awful personage like waxwork, and presently offering him at the reduced price of eighteen-pence. As I declined the proposal on the plea of an appointment, he was so good as to take me into a yard and show me where the gallows was kept, and also where people were publicly whipped, and then he showed me the Debtors' Door, out of which culprits came to be hanged; heightening the interest of that dreadful portal by giving me to understand that "four on 'em" would come out at that door the day after to-morrow at eight in the morning, to be killed in a row.

Soundscapes made in GarageBand

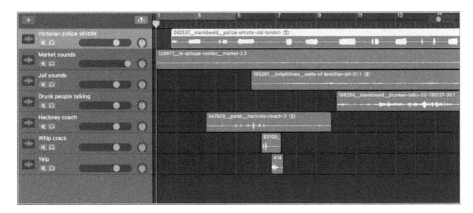

Available to listen and download from: https://leonfurze.files.wordpress.
com/2022/02/garageband-dickens-soundscape-example.mp3

Written explanation

I found the sounds on freesound.org. I used the market
sounds as the background to the whole soundscape because
it sounds as though there is a lot of activity happening.
Also, the text says 'Smithfield' and when I searched for
that I learned it is a market in London. For the other
sounds I arranged them in the order they appear in the
text. For example, the whip crack and the yelp happen about
halfway through to match the phrase, "people were publicly
whipped," in the second paragraph.

Reflect

I've run this activity with junior and senior students, and with very successful results. It can take a bit of time to set up – each student's technical capability is different, as is the quality of their device if your school has a 'bring your own' policy – but once students get the hang of it, it can be replicated across different scenes in a text, or a range of different texts.

When issues crop up with activities like this, simplify. Move to groups rather than individuals and try to make sure there's at least one tech-savvy student in each group. As stated in the introduction to the activity, you can also set up your own libraries ahead of time. If all else fails, you can even have the students record their own sounds rather than using stock audio.

- Could you make a soundscape for nonfiction texts as well as fiction? What details would you have students draw on?
- What happens if there's a catastrophic tech failure (not that the internet connection in schools ever fails...)? Can you reimagine this activity as a dramatic performance, with students layering up sounds vocally?

Extend

As with all of the activities in this book, it's always good to think of further written or discussion-based outcomes. As well as the brief written explanation, students could:

- Annotate the original text, identifying where their particular sounds enter/exit the soundscape
- Use their soundscape as the backing track for a new creative response, like an aural writing prompt
- Work in groups to discuss and share their soundscapes, and then develop a group soundscape, which further refines the visualisation of the text

ACTIVITY 3:
LINE-BY-LINE VISUALISATION

This activity encourages students to question a text from multiple angles, investigating not only the text itself, but also the context in which it was written.

Close reading often involves multiple readings of the same short extract or text. This activity provides a framework for those multiple readings.

Instructions for teachers

☑ An extract from a text with suitable details/description. Choose an extract that has enough visual or sensory information for students to be able to easily draw their 'mental image' of the scene. If possible, it may help to break the extract up line by line (see example) in sentences or clauses

☑ Pens and paper

☑ Space in the classroom to arrange students sitting back-to-back

1. Students must sit in pairs, back-to-back. In a small classroom, this might involve moving the furniture around to create enough space between pairs so that everyone can hear their partner.
2. Have the first partner read the extract aloud, pausing at the end of each sentence (or clauses/parts of sentences for texts with lengthy sentences) for around 10 seconds.
3. While the first partner reads aloud, the second should draw the scene as it unfolds. They can add to and amend their drawing as the reading progresses. Stress that the drawing doesn't have to be perfect, but it does need to capture the detail from the text.
4. Once the first partner has finished reading, switch roles. The two students are drawing a visualisation from the same extract.
5. At the end of the activity, the students should compare drawings and complete the short reflection.

Instructions for students

Sit back-to-back with your partner. Make sure that you can hear them speaking.

One student needs to read the extract line by line. The other must draw an image of what they are hearing. The picture doesn't have to be detailed, but it does have to reflect the text.

Once you've finished, swap roles.

After you have both drawn a visualisation, swap pictures and complete the reflection.

Example

From *The Great Gatsby* by F Scott Fitzgerald (NB: Line breaks indicate where students should pause.)

This is a valley of ashes—

a fantastic farm where ashes grow like wheat into ridges and hills and grotesque gardens;

where ashes take the forms of houses and chimneys and rising smoke and, finally, with a transcendent effort, of ash-grey men, who move dimly and already crumbling through the powdery air.

Occasionally a line of grey cars crawls along an invisible track, gives out a ghastly creak, and comes to rest, and immediately the ash-grey men swarm up with leaden spades and stir up an impenetrable cloud, which screens their obscure operations from your sight.

But above the grey land and the spasms of bleak dust which drift endlessly over it, you perceive, after a moment, the eyes of Doctor T. J. Eckleburg.

The eyes of Doctor T. J. Eckleburg are blue and gigantic—their retinas are one yard high.

They look out of no face, but, instead, from a pair of enormous yellow spectacles which pass over a nonexistent nose.

Evidently some wild wag of an oculist set them there to fatten his practice in the borough of Queens, and then sank down himself into eternal blindness, or forgot them and moved away.

But his eyes, dimmed a little by many paintless days, under sun and rain, brood on over the solemn dumping ground.

Student Visualisation drawings of the extract from *The Great Gatsby*

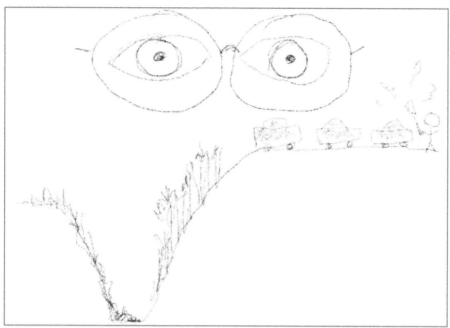

Reflection: What were the similarities and differences between your visualisation and your partner's?

I didn't realise that the Dr's eyes are on a billboard and not floating over the city! That makes more sense. Also you can see the traffic of grey cars in both of our drawings.

Reflect

The volume of this activity can quickly reach the 'leaving the classroom with a headache' range, so spacing the students out is a definite must. I've had students spilling out into the corridor for extra classroom space. You could also change up this activity by having students individually respond to a pre-recorded line-by-line reading, which has the advantage of being much quieter, but lacks some of the fun of collaboration.

- What is the advantage of running this activity line by line rather than reading the whole extract at once? Are there any possible advantages to doing it the other way around?
- The instructions call for an extract that is dense in visual or sensory imagery. Would/could this activity work with an extract that is lacking that kind of detail?
- How could you engage the other senses in this activity?

Extend

The drawings that students produce through this activity are a good basis for some focused discussion of key quotes in the text. You could have students 'annotate' their drawings by referring back to the original extract and labelling with quotes. Additionally:

- Use the quotes that produced the most vivid aspects of the drawing as the basis for a short text response.
- Use the drawing itself as a prompt for creative writing, or have students swap their drawings with another student so that *they* can use it as a prompt.
- Hold a discussion as a class to reach a consensus on the most important quotes from the extract, prompting students to explore *why* those quotes elicited such a strong response.

ACTIVITY 4: READING IN ROLE

Reading in Role is a fun activity that borrows techniques from the Drama classroom. In this instance I'm using the activity to target that 'sixth sense' of empathy. Having students empathise with the characters in texts not only encourages them to look at those characters in more detail, but also to consider the author's intent.

Instructions for teachers

☑ An extract from a text with suitable characterisation. Students should be able to identify something of the character's inner thoughts and feelings, either through their words, actions, the narrative or internal monologue
☑ Space to perform the role in pairs or small groups

1. Prepare for the performance by allowing time to read, annotate and plan. Students should prepare for this individually.
2. Divide students into pairs or small groups. Allow them time to rehearse, and then to perform their role in the pair/group.
3. Allow time at the end for students to complete the reflection.

Instructions for students

You will be performing a dramatic presentation of the character from this extract.

Read the extract carefully and make notes on how you might perform this role. For example, how will you move, what will you say? Will you speak out loud their inner thoughts?

Try to annotate the text with as much detail as possible to help your performance.

Rehearse and then perform the role in pairs/small groups.

Complete the short reflection task.

Example

From *Hard Times* by Charles Dickens

He was a rich man: banker, merchant, manufacturer, and what not. A big, loud man, with a stare, and a metallic laugh. A man made out of a coarse material, which seemed to have been stretched to make so much of him. A man with a great puffed head and forehead, swelled veins in his temples, and such a strained skin to his face that it seemed to hold his eyes open, and lift his eyebrows up. A man with a pervading appearance on him of being inflated like a balloon, and ready to start. A man who could never sufficiently vaunt himself a self-made man. A man who was always proclaiming, through that brassy speaking-trumpet of a voice of his, his old ignorance and his old poverty. A man who was the Bully of humility.

Think about posture. Prob stands up v straight with puffed out chest

Staring - big bulging eyes

Puffed out head!

He's a big man. Good detail. How do I act 'stretched'?

All the language about 'inflated' – more puffing up, walking around like I own the place

Think about posture. Prob stands up v straight with puffed out chest

Relection Task

What did you find easy about the performance?

There was a lot of physical detail, so it was easy to come up with actions for the character to show his big, inflated appearance.

What was difficult?

There was no dialogue or monologue, so I had to come up with a phrase of my own to show his trumpet voice.

What did you learn about how the author has chosen to portray this character?

Dickens placed a lot of emphasis on how the character was 'big', 'puffed', 'inflated' and 'swelled'. All of that detail in one short paragraph really makes it clear that he is not a likable character.

Reflect

Dramatic activities are a powerful way of getting students to engage with texts. Although it can sometimes be difficult to get out of the students' (and teacher's) comfort zones, it's definitely worthwhile. Don't limit dramatic activities like this to junior and middle school students, either. One of the most successful dramatisations I've seen came from a Year 12 class studying *Frankenstein*, focusing on the confrontation between Victor and his creation in the Swiss Alps. The performance was great, and the reflections that came from them even better.

♦ What other text types could this be used for? Scripts for dramatic pieces are an obvious choice, but what about nonfiction texts?
♦ If you have a cohort of students who are anxious about performing, what low-stakes warm-up activities could you use to get them into the performance? Think about speaking to your nearest handy Drama teacher for ideas.

Extend

Because dramatic performances engage multiple senses, they also stay in students' memories for longer. This makes this activity perfect for starting a character study and referring to throughout a unit, culminating in an analytical or creative response. You could also extend by:

- Having students perform to an audience, rather than as a group; members of the audience could also offer 'directorial' feedback on the performance
- Stitching together multiple performances, perhaps running the activity multiple times with different characters

.

CHAPTER 3

STRATEGY 3: QUESTIONING

When students ask questions – predicting, making assumptions, interrogating the text – they both demonstrate their current understanding and enhance future readings. Teaching students not just *why* to ask questions but also *how* provides them with a powerful tool that is a stepping stone towards complex inference and critical literacy skills.

All too often the classroom discourse is centred on teacher-led questioning. Reading is treated as an exercise in comprehension – we read the text to generate questions about what students have read. Unfortunately, this reductive method of teaching text produces several unfavourable outcomes. Firstly, it is difficult to assess whether individual students have understood the text. Some may volunteer answers, but many will remain silent. Secondly, asking students teacher-derived questions frames their reading of the text – readers are put into the position of having to search for the answer they think the teacher is looking for. Finally, and possibly most importantly, it is disengaging. Nothing kills reading faster than a battery of comprehension questions.

Creating opportunities for students to *ask* questions is much more rewarding. Mature readers reflexively ask questions while they read, building suppositions based on the information presented in the text. Students can be coached in the process of asking deep, meaningful questions that will open the text up to readings even the teacher could not have thought of.

Modelling Questions

Before using any of the activities that follow, it is a good idea to ensure that students understand *how* to ask questions. Activity 1: Four Questions addresses this through questions that are aligned with Bloom's taxonomy. However, it may also be useful to model question types as follows:

- Use Think Alouds to model your own questioning process. Read a text or extract as a class, perhaps projecting the extract for annotation. Model the kinds of questions *you* would think of while reading.
- Analyse and break down exam-style questions or essay prompts. Look for the different kinds of *task words* used such as 'discuss', 'explore' and so on.
- Whenever you read a text, model good questioning behaviours; remember that questions can be rhetorical and designed to provoke thoughts and discussion, rather than always needing an answer.

ACTIVITY 1:
FOUR QUESTIONS

This activity introduces students to four kinds of questions they might use when questioning texts. It uses Bloom's taxonomy (1956) and Dalton and Smith's (1986) work to scaffold questions of increasing complexity, demonstrating the importance of going beyond knowledge and comprehension-based questions.

Instructions for teachers

1. Arrange students in pairs or groups of three.
2. Explain the four types of questions as follows:
   a. **Knowledge and comprehension** questions ask for information, description, explanation and understanding
   b. **Application** questions ask us to show or illustrate knowledge
   c. **Analysis** questions ask us to examine, compare and analyse
   d. **Synthesising and evaluating** questions ask us to design, imagine, argue and justify
3. Provide the students with useful verbs and examples of the question types.
4. Instruct students to work together to write one of each level of question for a text/extract they have recently studied.

Instructions for students

Question Type	Useful Verbs	Example Questions
Knowledge and comprehension	Tell List Describe Find State Name Explain	What happens in the opening paragraph? Can you name the main character? True or false...? How many persuasive techniques does the author use in...? How would you describe the image? What do you think happens next?
Application	Show Illustrate Examine Solve	From the information given, can you solve the following...? Can you group together any of the techniques used by the impact on the reader? Do you know another instance where...? Can you draw a picture of the scene where...? What questions would you ask the character?
Analysis	Analyse Compare Contrast Investigate Explore	How is this scene similar to...? Why did... occur? What are the differences between this character and...? Where is the turning point in this chapter? What was the underlying theme of...? What is the major problem with...? How is... different to...?
Synthesising and evaluating	Create Invent Construct Design Imagine Justify Argue Discuss	Can you design a... based on this text? What would happen if...? If you were in this situation, how would you deal with...? What do you think about...? How would you feel if...? Which side of the argument do you agree with, and why?

Example

Student questions written about *Wonder* by RJ Palacio.

Question Type	Useful Verbs	Example Questions
Knowledge and comprehension	Tell List Describe Find State Name Explain	Who is the narrator of Part One of the book? How many characters have their own parts? What do you think will happen to August when he starts school?
Application	Show Illustrate Examine Solve	From the descriptions in the book, can you draw a family photograph of the Pullmans? Can you draw a web of the characters in this text? What clues in the first chapter suggest what is going to happen later in the book?
Analysis	Analyse Compare Contrast Investigate Explore	Have you ever read a book that tells the story from different perspectives? What happens at the climax of this novel? What is the main theme, issue or idea in Wonder?
Synthesising and evaluating	Create Invent Construct Design Imagine Justify Argue Discuss	If you were August, how would you have reacted to Daisy's death? Why is empathy important? The characters in Wonder all have their own personal battles. Discuss.

Reflect

Organising questions into a hierarchy makes it very clear to students that questioning is about more than just comprehension and understanding. All students, regardless of ability, can be encouraged to think more deeply about texts through effective questioning. I have modified this activity in the past by using colour-coded sentence starter cards, the colours indicating the different levels. Students are encouraged at first to try questions from the level they are comfortable with, and the next level up. After a while, students simply shuffle the deck of cards and choose at random.

◆ What is your 'default mode' when questioning students? Record yourself or have another teacher observe you and note the questions you ask. Do you range across the levels, or hover around one or two? Does it depend on the content of the lesson? Are your questions targeted at individual students, or designed for the whole class?
◆ What about the students? Do they have a default mode, too? If so, what can you do to explicitly develop their questioning skills?

Extend

The obvious way to extend this activity is to select some of the questions – at least one from each level – to answer in the class. This may involve students answering each other's questions or selecting four questions to answer as a group. You could also:

◆ Use questions as an 'exit pass'. Instead of getting students to *answer* questions on the way out of the door, get them to *ask*.
◆ Turn questions into assessable topics (see Activity 4: Deep Questions for more on this)
◆ Use questions as the basis for a Socratic seminar – the taxonomy structure is perfect for this popular discussion activity

ACTIVITY 2: WHY? WHY? WHY?

The Why? Why? Why? questioning activity encourages students to go deeper, searching for meaning beyond a superficial reading of the text. Initial responses to text are often surface level, and students often want to write the first response that comes into their head and then move on quickly so that the work is 'done'. This activity ensures students dwell on a text to produce a more robust reading.

Instructions for teachers

1. Begin with a reading of a text or an extract of a text. The text could be read aloud as a class or individually. Students do not need to annotate the text on the first reading.
2. After reading the text, write a simple declarative statement about the text on the board. This might be a statement such as: 'The character Bernice is angry' or 'An important value in this extract is justice'.
3. Instruct students to form a 'Why...?' question around the statement. For example, 'Why is Bernice angry?' or 'Why is justice important in this extract?'
4. Have students swap their questions with a partner. In pairs, the students should attempt to answer the first 'Why?'
5. The students should now derive a second 'Why...?' question based on the answer their partner provided. For example, if the student responded, 'Bernice is angry because she has been undermined', an appropriate second question would be 'Why was she undermined?'
6. Repeat steps 5 and 6 a third and final time.
7. Have students write a summary sentence of their three 'Whys'.

Instructions for students

Complete the following table, starting with the statement based on the text you have just read:

Statement (by teacher)	
First 'Why...?'	
First answer	
Second 'Why...?'	
Second answer	
Third 'Why...?'	
Third answer	

Summary sentence

_____

_____

_____

Example

From *Alice's Adventures in Wonderland* by Lewis Carroll

Alice was beginning to get very tired of sitting by her sister on the bank, and of having nothing to do: once or twice she had peeped into the book her sister was reading, but it had no pictures or conversations in it, "and what is the use of a book," thought Alice "without pictures or conversations?"

So she was considering in her own mind (as well as she could, for the hot day made her feel very sleepy and stupid), whether the pleasure of making a daisy-chain would be worth the trouble of getting up and picking the daisies, when suddenly a White Rabbit with pink eyes ran close by her.

There was nothing so very remarkable in that; nor did Alice think it so very much out of the way to hear the Rabbit say to itself, "Oh dear! Oh dear! I shall be late!" (when she thought it over afterwards, it occurred to her that she ought to have wondered at this, but at the time it all seemed quite natural); but when the Rabbit actually took a watch *out of its waistcoat-pocket*, and looked at it, and then hurried on, Alice started to her feet, for it flashed across her mind that she had never before seen a rabbit with either a waistcoat-pocket, or a watch to take out of it, and burning with curiosity, she ran across the field after it, and fortunately was just in time to see it pop down a large rabbit-hole under the hedge.

Student statements written about *Alice's Adventures in Wonderland* by Lewis Carroll

Statement (by teacher)	Lewis Carroll creates a feeling of unreality right from the start of *Alice's Adventures in Wonderland*.
First 'Why...?'	Why does Carroll create a sense of unreality from the very start?
First answer	To set up the rest of Alice's adventures.
Second 'Why...?'	Why does Carroll need to set up the rest of Alice's adventures?
Second answer	Because lots of strange things will happen to her.
Third 'Why...?'	Why do lots of strange things happen to her?
Third answer	Because Wonderland is a very strange place.

Summary sentence

Lewis Carroll creates a sense of unreality from the very start of Alice's Adventures in Wonderland because Wonderland is a very strange place, and lots of strange things are about to happen to Alice.

Reflect

Compare the final example to the student's initial response, 'to set up the rest of Alice's adventures'. The final response incorporates more detail and offers a solid base for a deeper reading of the text. Going down the rabbit hole (*Alice* pun intended) leads to a much more thoughtful response and will even help with 'I don't know what to write' syndrome. Once a student has come up with a few layers of 'why', they have already paved the way for a longer response. The activity affords them more thinking time to digest the initial prompt and discourages the knee-jerk reactions, which lead to generic, one-sided responses.

- When you give students a prompt, how much time do you spend unpacking the prompt and how do you go about it? Do you annotate as a class? Is there discussion?
- Try the activity for yourself before doing it with a class. If you can't think of enough 'layers' to your response, perhaps the prompt needs changing.
- Think about how this activity could be applied to creative writing as well as expository/analytical. How would the three 'Whys' structure work with a writing prompt like *Seamus was in a bad mood that day?*

Extend

There may be opportunities to extend this task by drawing links between the students' final sentences and literary techniques, thematic concerns, values and so on. To extend this activity:

- Share summary sentences as a class. Write examples up on the board and draw comparisons, indicating the similarities and differences between students' readings.
- Draw out technical terms implied in student readings. In the *Alice* example above, this student's response sets up perfectly an introduction to *foreshadowing*.
- Use summary sentences as a topic for a longer paragraph, or as a model for a sentence in a longer paragraph.

ACTIVITY 3:
TEXT INTERROGATION

This activity encourages students to question a text from multiple angles, investigating not only the text itself, but also the context in which it was written.

Close reading often involves multiple readings of the same short extract or text. This activity provides a framework for those multiple readings.

Instructions for teachers

1. This activity can be completed individually or in pairs/groups.
2. Begin with a reading of the text. Discuss with students the idea that texts are produced by authors in a specific *context* – the 'who, what, when, where, why' of a text's production.
3. Guide students through the steps of the task. Stop the lesson at timed intervals to reflect on the steps and get feedback from the students on their work.
4. Step one: The broad context – What was happening in the world when this text was produced and when it is set? What global, national and local issues may have impacted on the text's production?
5. Step two: The author's context – Who wrote the text? What other things have they written? What biases might they have?
6. Step three: The issues, values and ideas – What issues, values and ideas are present in the text? How do they relate to the broader context, and the author's context?

Instructions for students

Reading a text sometimes involves looking beyond the words on the page and digging deeper into the author and the world around them. Use the framework to interrogate the text from different angles.

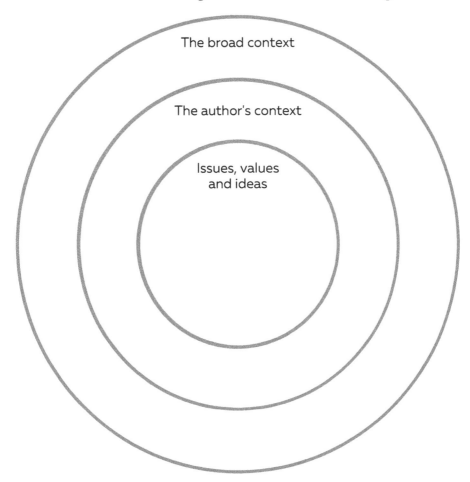

The broad context – What was happening in the world when this text was produced and when it is set? What global, national and local issues may have impacted on the text's production?

The author's context – Who wrote the text? What other things have they written? What biases might they have?

The issues, values and ideas – What issues, values and ideas are present in the text? How do they relate to the broader context, and the author's context?

Example

Text Interrogation for *The Midnight Zoo* by Sonya Hartnett

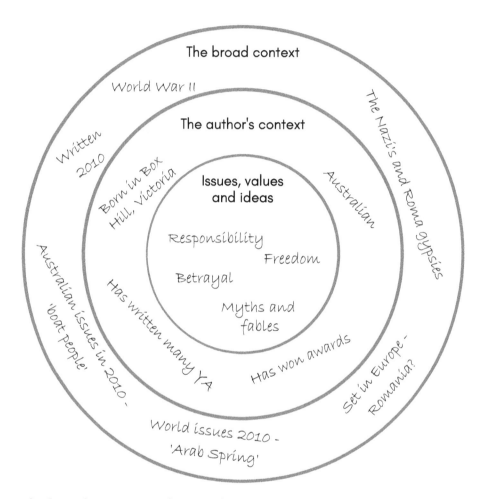

The broad context

World War II

The Nazi's and Roma gypsies

Written 2010

The author's context

Born in Box Hill, Victoria

Australian

Issues, values and ideas

Responsibility

Freedom

Betrayal

Myths and fables

Australian issues in 2010 - 'boat people'

Has written many YA

Has won awards

Set in Europe - Romania?

World issues 2010 - 'Arab Spring'

The broad context – What was happening in the world when this text was produced and when it is set? What global, national and local issues may have impacted on the text's production?

The author's context – Who wrote the text? What other things have they written? What biases might they have?

The issues, values and ideas – What issues, values and ideas are present in the text? How do they relate to the broader context, and the author's context?

Reflect

Text Interrogation sits nicely alongside other contextualising activities like the Context Walk from Chapter 1: Making Connections. As discussed there, it isn't the job of the English teacher to spend hours discussing the historical, social and political contexts of a text, as much as we might like to. You could use this activity immediately following the Context Walk, which could provide students with more than enough material to fill the outer two circles. Consider:

- How much context is too much? When should you draw the line with providing context to the texts you are studying?
- *When* should you study context? At the beginning, to support understanding, or at the end, so that it doesn't colour the students' interpretations?
- How should students express their knowledge of context? In the introduction to an essay? Throughout? Does context have a place at all in a text response? Or should it just sit in the background of their understanding?

Extend

Unlike the other questioning activities in this chapter, the Text Interrogation provides students with explicit questions to respond to. This does not mean that students cannot produce their own questions.

- Using the notes from inside each of the circles, have students generate a list of follow-up questions to go deeper into the context of the text.
- Conduct a fishbowl discussion based on one of the circles.

ACTIVITY 4: DEEP QUESTIONS

When we provide students with end-of-topic questions – examination topics, written assessment tasks, coursework – we design them to be complex, deep questions. Encouraging students to write their own deep questions is a great indicator of knowledge, and a way of collaborating on those final tasks.

This activity is best completed after students have tried the other three activities so that they have an awareness of the four levels of questioning, the importance of asking 'Why?' more than once, and an appreciation of the impact of context on a text.

Instructions for teachers

1. Complete this task at the end of a text study or unit of work. This task may be completed individually or in pairs.
2. Find key moments in the text. In a larger text, these may be turning points, moments of conflict and so on. In a shorter text, such as a poem, this could encompass the entire text.
3. Have students brainstorm a list of five to 10 questions about the key moments. The questions should be from the analysis or synthesis and evaluation levels of questioning.
4. Ask students to select their 'best question'. In turn, students read the questions aloud and the teacher transcribes into a shared document.
5. As a class, review the questions. Categorise them into, for example: themes, issues and ideas; character based; context based. Highlight any questions students may have offered that fall outside the required categories and discuss how to improve them.
6. Select and discuss the questions the class believes are the richest.

Instructions for students

Brainstorm a list of five to 10 questions about the key moment(s) you have chosen.

The questions should be from the analysis or synthesis and evaluation levels of questioning.

Example

From *Frankenstein* by Mary Shelley

"When night came I quitted my retreat and wandered in the wood; and now, no longer restrained by the fear of discovery, I gave vent to my anguish in fearful howlings. I was like a wild beast that had broken the toils, destroying the objects that obstructed me and ranging through the wood with a stag-like swiftness. Oh! What a miserable night I passed! The cold stars shone in mockery, and the bare trees waved their branches above me; now and then the sweet voice of a bird burst forth amidst the universal stillness. All, save I, were at rest or in enjoyment; I, like the arch-fiend, bore a hell within me, and finding myself unsympathised with, wished to tear up the trees, spread havoc and destruction around me, and then to have sat down and enjoyed the ruin...

..."My travels were long and the sufferings I endured intense. It was late in autumn when I quitted the district where I had so long resided. I travelled only at night, fearful of encountering the visage of a human being. Nature decayed around me, and the sun became heatless; rain and snow poured around me; mighty rivers were frozen; the surface of the earth was hard and chill, and bare, and I found no shelter. Oh, earth! How often did I imprecate curses on the cause of my being! The mildness of my nature had fled, and all within me was turned to gall and bitterness. The nearer I approached to your habitation, the more deeply did I feel the spirit of revenge enkindled in my heart. Snow fell, and the waters were hardened, but I rested not. A few incidents now and then directed me, and I possessed a map of the country; but I often wandered wide from my path. The agony of my feelings allowed me no respite; no incident occurred from which my rage and misery could not extract its food; but a circumstance that happened when I arrived on the confines of Switzerland, when the sun had recovered its warmth and the earth again began to look green, confirmed in an especial manner the bitterness and horror of my feelings...

Examples of student-generated deep questions

- What does the monster burning down the cottage represent?
- "No longer restrained by the fear of discovery" – does this mean the monster has now come to terms with his true self?
- Is the monster like this because of nurture or nature?
- That burst all bounds of reason and reflection" – why did Shelley blame the monster's reaction on nature?
- Why does the monster become despised by humanity just because he is ugly or looks different?
- "You my creator would tear me to pieces in time... why should I pity man more than he pities me?" – why should the monster pity mankind?
- The monster says, "I too can create desolation" – what other desolations is he referring to?
- Why does the monster crave human acceptance?

Reflect

This is an excellent activity for senior English and works very well as a precursor to School Assessed Coursework and exam-style responses. At the end of a unit of work, getting students to frame their own questions is – in my opinion – much more useful than simply providing them with a list. Stepping into the shoes of the examination setting panel is always a good idea and can also help to identify 'blind spots', where students have gaps in their knowledge of the key issues, values and ideas of a text.

- How could you combine this activity with some of the others, for example, Four Questions?
- What would need to happen to make it more accessible for junior levels? How could you scaffold or model the process further to support students?

Extend

Again, the logical next step for this activity is to produce a written outcome. If the students are not yet at the stage where they're ready for a full written piece, you might consider:

- Selecting one or more of the questions to work through as a class, developing a plan or outline for a response
- Repeating the activity with another key moment, and drawing links
- Repeating the activity with a second text, and drawing links to the first

CHAPTER 4

STRATEGY 4: INFERRING

Inferring means 'reading between the lines'. In practice, however, it's one of the most complex Reading Strategies for a student to access and requires a much more sophisticated understanding of text than simple comprehension. I discussed in the introduction that these Strategies are not hierarchical, but it certainly makes sense to build students' confidence with close reading through Making Connections, Visualising and Questioning before asking them to make inferences. The other Strategies will provide students with methods to tackle these more complex activities.

Although inference is complex, it is – like many processes – formed early in a child's development. Studies have shown that children as young as three years old can begin to infer information from stories, such as conflict, plot and character arcs (Filiatrault-Veilleux, Bouchard, Trudeau & Desmarais, 2015). Similarly, children can begin to conceptualise the difference between real and imaginary information from four years old, with a lot of skill development between four and six (Tullos & Woolley, 2009). Even so, the prevalence of 'fake news' and the communication of misleading information on social media proves that even though we can infer from an early age, we don't always choose to read between the lines before hitting the share button.

Inference, then, is a valuable skill for critical literacy, which is covered in more depth in part two of this book. It is a tool for decoding text that is developed in early childhood, but a tool that must be regularly sharpened. These activities sharpen the tool of inference, making use of both explicit and implicit information in texts to encourage the reader to look beyond the obvious, question their first assumptions and approach texts with a critical eye.

ACTIVITY 1:
QUOTE – PARAPHRASE –
CONNECTION – INFERENCE

All too often, students can identify a quote in a text, which 'looks good', but they are unable to explain the relevance of the quote in light of a given topic or prompt. This may partially be because writing about quotes directly attempts to short-circuit some of the inference needed to explore the evidence in context.

For many students, it is difficult to articulate exactly *why* a quote is important. This activity slows down the process of explaining a quote, beginning with a paraphrase, then connecting the quote to the broader text or extract, and finally making an inference.

Instructions for teachers

☑ An extract from the text currently being studied, or a copy of an entire short text

☑ OR a collection of quotes the student has already identified from the text

☑ A copy of the Quote – Paraphrase – Connection – Inference (QPCI) table, in print or digital form

1. This activity can be carried out on a text/extract that has not yet been studied, or as a method of improving the discussion of quotes that students have already found. If the text has not been studied yet, provide students with a copy, and time to annotate. Prompt students with a simple instruction to "underline any words or phrases that you believe are important" or provide a specific prompt to work around.

2. Once students have identified a number of quotes from the text, ask them to transfer the quotes to the first column of the table. These

can be single words or short phrases, but steer students away from copying out lengthy passages.

3. In the paraphrase column, students should summarise each quote in their own words. For single-word quotes, this means writing their own definition and/or synonyms. For phrases, students should reword the quote. See Activity 2: Key Idea Paraphrase in the Summarising chapter if students are unfamiliar with paraphrasing.

4. In the connection column, students should connect the quote to any of the following:
   a. Other points from the text
   b. Their own knowledge (text-to-self)
   c. Other texts (text-to-text)
   d. The world around them (text-to-world)

5. In the final column, inference, students should make a claim based on their understanding of the quote. For example, this could be a statement about the author's views or values, about a character's motivation, about the speaker's beliefs and so on.

Instructions for students

Annotate the text/extract looking for words or phrases you think may be important (key quotes).

Transfer the quotes to the left column of the table.

In the **paraphrase** column, restate the quote in your own words. For example, define the word or summarise the phrase.

In the **connection** column, make a connection with the quote, for example, text-to-self, text-to-text, text-to-world, or connect to another part of the same text.

In the **inference** column, make a statement about the quote that shows your understanding of its meaning and importance. For example, what are the author's values? What is the character trying to say here?

Example

From *Othello* by William Shakespeare

Quotation	Paraphrase	Connection	Inference
Iago: "I am not what I am." (1.1)	Iago is deliberately deceptive.	Later in the play, Othello calls him "honest Iago".	From the very start of the play, Iago makes it clear that he is deceptive, which allows Shakespeare to highlight his many dishonest and manipulative actions.
Emilia (to Desdemona about men): "They are all but stomachs, and we all but food..." (3.4)	Men eat us up.	Reminds me of media coverage of the #MeToo movement, which exposed how many men abused their positions of power and mistreated women.	Shakespeare's metaphor about the relationship between men and women shows an imbalance of power.
Othello (about himself): "...one that loved not wisely, but too well..." (5.2)	Othello loved Desdemona too much.	Links to the quote above.	Othello's love is consuming, and he uses it as an excuse for murdering Desdemona.

Reflect

Slowing down the reading of a text can be daunting, especially in a system that has typically favoured content over skills and a busy curriculum. Even so, we must take the time to slow down and allow students to grapple with quotes. The example above, taken from a

Literature study of *Othello*, demonstrates the increased sophistication of a student's response when given just a little more time to focus on the inference.

Often, students will reach the first point – the paraphrase – and then move on, for example, writing something like, "Othello's claim that he 'loved not wisely, but too well', means that he loved Desdemona too much." This demonstrates an *understanding* of the quote, but does not infer any deeper meaning from it.

- How often do we ask students to write about quotes – either in sentences, paragraphs or full essays – without giving time to truly explore the quote and its meaning?
- How could you scaffold this process further for struggling students? Modelling parts of the process, supporting through class or peer discussion?
- Would the QPCI activity work for other forms, such as film or multimodal text analysis? What would you change?

Extend

The QPCI activity obviously points towards analytical writing. To extend the activity:

- Have students do a think-pair-share or group discussion around their inferences. Multiple interpretations often create a richer interpretation.
- Discuss inferences as a class and sort/categorise them, for example, thematically, by character, by the part of the text the quotes were taken from.
- Use the 'I' column to form the basis of an essay. Think about the impact this would have on essay planning as opposed to other methods, such as TEEL.

ACTIVITY 2:
READ BETWEEN THE LINES

In the introduction to this chapter, I referred to inference as 'reading between the lines'. This activity makes that literal, by encouraging students to infer into each line of text. Inferences are made based on experience and evidence, so again it would be useful if students have encountered some of the Making Connections, Questioning and Visualising activities prior to this.

Instructions for teachers

☑ An extract from the text currently being studied, double-line spaced

1. Prepare the extract by double-line spacing on a single A4 sheet. Choose an extract (or allow students to choose their own), which is rich enough to undertake a line-by-line analysis. This activity would be perfect for poetry.
2. Discuss the annotation process with students; they are to move through the text line by line, and underneath each line write a single sentence exploring the meaning of the preceding line. This meaning could, for example, come from:
    a. Making connections: text-to-self, text-to-text, text-to-world
    b. Asking questions/interrogating the text
    c. Visualisations, such as exploring the use of sensory language and imagery
    d. Observations about the author's meaning, intent or purpose
3. Allow time for the students to complete the line-by-line analysis.

Instructions for students

The text has been broken up line by line. Read each line, and below it add your own notes about any *meaning* you read into the text. This meaning could come from:

♦ Making connections: text-to-self, text-to-text, text-to-world
♦ Asking questions/interrogating the text
♦ Visualisations, such as exploring the use of sensory language and imagery
♦ Observations about the author's meaning, intent or purpose

Example

From 'I Wandered Lonely as a Cloud' (commonly known as 'Daffodils') by William Wordsworth

I wandered lonely as a cloud

Wandering is pointless, aimless. Cloud backs up the 'lonely' image.

That floats on high o'er vales and hills,

Floats makes me think of the 'wandering' – sort of floating around aimlessly.

When all at once I saw a crowd,

Sudden, surprising.

A host, of golden daffodils;

'Crowd' and 'host' are unusual words to use for flowers. Makes them sound like people. Personification.

Beside the lake, beneath the trees,

This reminds me of a kid's book 'bears in the night'!

Fluttering and dancing in the breeze.

He's wandering aimlessly, but the flowers are fluttering and dancing and having fun. More personification.

Reflect

Although this activity works particularly well with poetry, it can be applied to any text type. Some texts will have more layers of meaning than others, and often, students will not begin to infer meaning until they are a few sentences in. It's fine, therefore, if the first few lines of their analysis are a little sparse.

- How would this activity look with a persuasive text? What kinds of meaning – such as identifying appeals and techniques – could students look for?
- Do students need to be able to infer meaning from every line of text? Or is it more important that they build towards an overall inference. Does it depend on the text type?

Extend

If students are able to derive meaning from every line – such as in a poem where the information may be 'denser' than in prose – then it is a good idea to finish this task with some sort of synthesis. The final chapter in part one has four synthesising activities, which could be applied to the text, or you could extend in the following ways:

- A discussion of students' different interpretations. It is always a good idea to see different perspectives on the same text.
- Pulling the separate lines of analysis into a single paragraph, making sure that it is edited for cohesion and not just a string of separate sentences copied into the shape of a paragraph!
- Read the text aloud a second time, pausing at the end of each line and allowing a different student to offer their interpretation.

ACTIVITY 3: MEANING MAP

This concept-mapping activity encourages students to dig a little deeper than just identifying *what* they see in the text and asks them to articulate *why* they have made that judgement. It can be a simple activity or one that extends into a very complex and detailed concept map at the end of a text study. This activity relies on the students knowing enough about the text to make several inferences, meaning that it is best suited for the end of a unit, or after a significant portion of the text has been read.

Instructions for teachers

☑ A text that has been studied in class
☑ A3 paper or butcher's paper and pens, or a digital canvas such as a slide or doc

1. Discuss the purpose of the Meaning Map with students; they will be making a concept map (mind map, brainstorm) of all of the deeper meanings in the text. These might be phrased as questions ('what is the meaning of life?', 'is it important to be kind?') or statements ('good will triumph over evil', 'rights must be protected') or themes and values ('justice', 'equality', 'truth').
2. Working in pairs, students should place all of the different meanings of the text around the central part of the map, leaving enough space around each element. Most complex texts will have multiple layers of meaning.
3. Meanings can be expanded further by breaking them down, for example, if one 'meaning' of the text is 'rights must be protected', the next level might break these down into different rights, such as 'freedom of speech', 'human rights', 'the right to life' and so on.
4. The final level of the Meaning Map should be evidence from the text. This could include direct quotes or paraphrases. Encourage students to include page numbers for longer texts.

Instructions for students

This mind-mapping activity encourages you to explore all of the layers of meaning in a text. Working in pairs, write down the different meanings or messages from the text.

For example, these might be phrased as questions ('what is the meaning of life?', 'is it important to be kind?') or statements ('good will triumph over evil', 'rights must be protected') or themes and values ('justice', 'equality', 'truth').

In the next level of the map, break down those meanings further. For example, if one 'meaning' of the text is 'rights must be protected', the next level might break these down into different rights, such as 'freedom of speech', 'human rights', 'the right to life' and so on.

The final level of the Meaning Map should be evidence from the text. This could include direct quotes or paraphrases. Encourage students to include page numbers for longer texts.

Example

Student mind-mapping activity

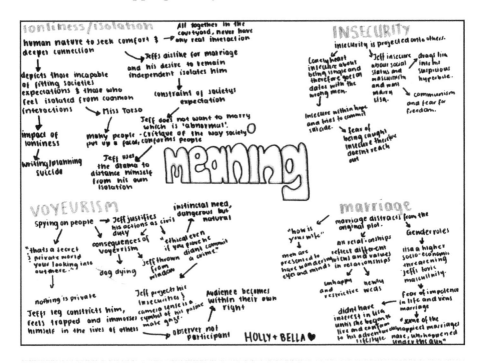

Reflect

Encouraging students to look more closely at the themes, issues and values in a text is an important skill for analysis. The senior English curriculum devotes a lot of time to writing analytical responses to texts, but frequently the skills of inference required to produce these essays are skimmed over in the rush to 'finish the book'. In my experience, it is far better to allow students more time to explore the ideas in the text than aiming directly for the final essay and trying to 'fill the gaps' in their knowledge by providing them with a list of key quotes and themes.

- What are the barriers to students inferring their own meanings from texts, rather than being led to them by the teacher?
- What can be done to overcome those barriers, other than explicitly telling the students what the key issues, themes and values are? For example, through class discussion, wider reading, support materials.
- Why is it important that students make their own meaning from texts?

Extend

This is another task that lends itself directly to the analytical essay. Concept mapping of any sort is a great way of encouraging students to clarify and expand on their ideas before writing. You could also extend this task in the following ways:

- Ask students to write their own examination-style questions based on the separate areas of their maps.
- Use those student-generated questions as the actual assessment questions, rather than assigning them yourself.
- Collate the Meaning Maps of all of the students and produce a class map of the text as a reference material.

ACTIVITY 4:
HOW DO THEY FEEL?
HOW DO YOU KNOW?

Empathising with characters in texts involves inference, particularly when authors show information rather than *telling* it. This means that students must be able to 'read between the lines' in order to understand a character's motivations, their actions and their relationships with other characters.

This activity asks students to identify moments in the text where a character is obviously feeling a certain emotion, and to demonstrate the inferences they have made.

Instructions for teachers

☑ A text that has been studied in class

1. This activity works best once enough of the text has been studied for students to see a character in a range of situations. Begin by discussing ways in which authors can *show* rather than *tell* how their characters feel, such as:
   a. Through their actions
   b. Through their behaviour in a situation
   c. Through their interactions and relationships
   d. Through dialogue
2. Ask students to identify moments in the text where the character is clearly *feeling* something. It may be useful to provide students with a list of emotion words for them to refer to. A quick search online will provide many lists. Students should aim to find four different feelings.
3. In the second column, students should identify how the author has portrayed the character's emotion.

4. In the third column, students should include a direct quote or a paraphrase from the text.

Instructions for students

Choose a character from your text. Find moments in the text where the character is obviously experiencing a strong feeling or emotion.

What is the feeling?

What is the author doing to show that character's feeling?

Include a quote or paraphrase.

Example

From *Laurinda* by Alice Pung

Character: Lucy

How do they feel?	How do you know?	Quote/Paraphrase
Excitement	☑ Actions ☑ Behaviour ☐ Interactions ☐ Dialogue ☐ Other	I think I must have made a sound like eeeek, eeeek, eeeek! because Mum came rushing into the house thinking the smoke alarm had gone off. p. 18
Embarrassment	☐ Actions ☑ Behaviour ☐ Interactions ☐ Dialogue ☐ Other	Not a thread of my new uniform had been in the wash. My shirt had crease lines from being folded in the packet... No one wore the blue hair ribbons – I was the only one dumb enough to have taken that part of the uniform code seriously. p. 39

Anger	☐ Actions ☐ Behaviour ☑ Interactions ☑ Dialogue ☐ Other	...I couldn't be bothered arguing with him. "We'll see," I said, to shut him up. p. 139
Embarrassment	☐ Actions ☐ Behaviour ☐ Interactions ☐ Dialogue ☑ Other	It was all bull, and I saw red. I'd been a leader before, and I knew it was not this rubbish about how everyone could be one if only they participated in enough public-speaking, merit-scoring activities. p. 329

Reflect

Getting students to empathise with a character can be hard work. First, you have to convince them to read enough of the book to get into the character's head. Then, you have to encourage them to read with the character's thoughts and feelings in mind, and not just through the lens of their own world view. On top of that, the text itself has to be well written enough that the reader can truly connect with the character. But when a student can empathise with a character, they find that the text suddenly makes sense, and the skill of inference – one of the most difficult skills in reading – suddenly becomes a lot easier.

- This activity is geared around fiction. How could you change it to focus on a nonfiction piece, such as empathising with the author of an opinion piece?
- How could you adjust this activity so that the students are encouraged to empathise with the author, and not the characters?
- Why is empathy an important skill for inference?

Extend

This activity can lead to both analytical and creative writing in a number of ways, for example:

- Use the quotes to write an analytical piece about the character, or about a theme, issue or value that the character represents.
- Use the emotions as a prompt for an original piece of creative writing, perhaps even using the quotes and paraphrases as models.
- Group students together and have them discuss the difference between portraying a character's emotions through actions, behaviours, interactions and dialogue.

CHAPTER 5

STRATEGY 5: SUMMARISING

Summarising involves recalling the main events or ideas from a text. The Strategy also extends to more sophisticated processes such as evaluating – passing judgement on the value of a text – and paraphrasing.

In order to summarise, students must be able to first read and comprehend the information in front of them. A summary is not a recount or carbon copy of the material. That means that students *must* engage with the text if they are to provide a successful summary.

Summary is important for *integrating* the main ideas in a text, taking them on board and making them a part of the understanding of the entire text. As such, it is a necessary stepping stone on the way to the final Strategy: synthesising. But summarising is also a valuable skill in its own right.

Summarising skills are used in a variety of text types, including:

- Reviews
- Persuasive arguments

- Blurbs
- Abstracts for academic articles
- Presentations

Paraphrasing versus summarising

Although included in this Strategy, paraphrasing and summarising are distinct skills. Think of paraphrasing as another half step towards synthesising. In a paraphrase, the student takes the key information they may use in a summary and expresses the meaning in their own words.

Paraphrasing allows students to include evidence from other texts or arguments in a style that fits the rest of their writing, making the writing much more fluent and coherent. A good paraphrase is often simpler and more concise than the text it is paraphrasing, allowing students to refine and articulate the key ideas.

Evaluating

In some instances, summarising may lead naturally to an evaluation of the text. This might be an evaluation of the quality, such as in a book or film review. Or it may be the evaluation of the success of an argument, or of the various merits of a piece of research. Summarising before evaluating is an important step as it allows students to process the information more fully before passing judgement.

Being able to evaluate texts allows students to make recommendations and to reflect on the qualities of work with increasing abstraction, such as making judgements of the values in a particular text (Derewianka & Jones, 2016). This then leads towards higher-order skills such as comparison and synthesis.

ACTIVITY 1: GUIDED SUMMARY

This initial activity guides students through the process of summarising a text. It works for any type of text, fiction or nonfiction, long or short. Initially, provide clear, modelled instruction on the process, particularly the first few stages. As students become more confident with their own summarising skills, gradually release the responsibility of the summarising to them. Ultimately, you are aiming to routinise summary so that students almost always summarise while they are reading complex texts.

Instructions for teachers

☑ The text that is to be summarised
☑ Pens or pencils
☑ A copy of the summarising guide (to be gradually phased out)

1. Begin by explaining all of the steps and the importance of summarising a text. Students should understand that summary is more than simply copying out the main points of a text.
2. If you are introducing this task for the first time, model steps 1 and 2 clearly: Step 1: Underline passages that contain main ideas. Step 2: Write a list of the main ideas.
3. As a class, or in pairs if the students are more confident, move on to Step 3: Combine similar ideas together.
4. Discuss Step 4: Organise the list of main ideas into order of importance.
5. Again, model this process with students if you are introducing them to the task or allow them to work in pairs if they are more confident.
6. Instruct students to complete Step 5: Write out the summary as a paragraph. This should be attempted individually.
7. Compare student responses.

Instructions for students

Step 1: Underline or highlight the parts of the text that contain the main ideas.

Step 2: Write out a list of the main ideas.

Step 3: Combine any similar ideas together.

Step 4: Organise your list of ideas into order of importance, with the most important ideas at the top of the list.

Step 5: Write your summary as a paragraph. The paragraph should contain the most important information from the text.

Guided Summary

Step 1: Underline or highlight the parts of the text that contain the main ideas

Step 2: Write out a list of the main ideas	
Step 3: Combine any similar ideas together	
Step 4: Organise your list of ideas into order of importance, with the most important ideas at the top of the list	
Step 5: Write your summary as a paragraph. The paragraph should contain the most important information from the text	

Example

From The Conversation website by Mark Boulet

Want to reduce your food waste at home? Here are the six best evidence-based ways to do it

Mark Boulet

Research Fellow, BehaviourWorks Australia, Monash University

September 29, 2021 6.10am AEST

From the farm to the plate, the modern day food system has a waste problem. Each year, a third of all food produced around the world, or 1.3 billion tonnes, ends up as rubbish. Imagine that for a moment – it's like buying three bags of groceries at the supermarket then throwing one away as you leave.

Wasting food feeds climate change. Food waste accounts for more than 5% of Australia's greenhouse gas emissions. And this doesn't include emissions from activities required to actually produce the food in the first place, such as farming and transport.

One of the largest sites of food waste is the home. In Australia, households throw out about 2.5 million tonnes of food each year. That equates to between A$2,000 and $2,500 worth of food per year per household.

But there's some good news. Our Australian-first research, released today, identified the six most effective behaviours anyone can do to reduce food waste. Combined, these relatively small changes can make a big difference.

What we did

Food waste by households is a complex problem influenced by many factors. Some, such as food type, package size and safety standards, are out of a consumer's control. But some are insignificant daily behaviours we can easily change, such as buying too much, forgetting about food at the back of your fridge, not eating leftovers and cooking too much food.

We wanted to better understand the complex nature of household food waste. Together with Australia's leading food rescue organisation OzHarvest, our research sought to identify and prioritise evidence-based actions to reduce the amount of food Australians throw away.

We reviewed Australian and international literature, and held online workshops with 30 experts, to collate a list of 36 actions to reduce food waste. These actions can be broadly grouped into: planning for shopping, shopping, storing food at home, cooking and eating.

We realised this might be an overwhelming number of behaviours to think about, and many people wouldn't know where to start. So we then surveyed national and international food waste experts, asking them to rank behaviours based on their impact in reducing food waste.

We also surveyed more than 1,600 Australian households. For each behaviour, participants were asked about:

- the amount of thinking and planning involved (mental effort)

- how much it costs to undertake the behaviour (financial effort)

- household "fit" (effort involved in adopting the behaviour based on different schedules and food preferences in the household).

Consumers identified mental effort as the most common barrier to reducing food waste.

What we found

Our research identified the three top behaviours with the highest impact in reducing food waste, which are also relatively easy to implement:

- Prepare a weekly meal at home that combines food needing to be used up
- Designate a shelf in the fridge or pantry for foods that need to be used up
- Before cooking a meal, check who in the household will be eating, to ensure the right amount is cooked.

Despite these actions being relatively easy, we found few Australian consumers had a "use it up" shelf in the fridge or pantry, or checked how many household members will be eating before cooking a meal.

Experts considered a weekly "use-it-up" meal to be the most effective behaviour in reducing food waste. Many consumers reported they already did this at home, but there is plenty of opportunity for others to adopt it.

Some consumers are more advanced players who have already included the above behaviours in their usual routines at home. So for those people, our research identified a further three behaviours requiring slightly more effort:

- Conduct an audit of weekly food waste and set reduction goals
- Make a shopping list and stick to it when shopping
- Make a meal plan for the next three to four days.

Our research showed a number of actions which, while worthwhile for many reasons, experts considered less effective at reducing food waste. They were also less likely to be adopted by consumers. The actions included:

- Preserving perishable foods by pickling, saucing or stewing for later use
- Making a stock of any food remains (bones and peels) and freeze for future use
- Buying food from local specialty stores (such as greengrocers and butchers) rather than large supermarkets.

Doing our bit

Today is the United Nations' International Day of Awareness of Food Loss and Waste. It seeks to increase awareness and prompt action in support of a key target in the global Sustainable Development Goals to halve food loss and waste by 2030.

Australia has signed up to this goal, and we hope this research helps fast-track those efforts.

OzHarvest is launching its national Use-It-Up food waste campaign today, aiming to support Australians with information, resources and tips. Based on our findings, we've also developed a decision-making tool to help policy makers target appropriate food waste behaviours.

Australia, and the world, can stop throwing away perfectly edible food – but everyone must play their part.

Guided Summary

Step 1: Underline or highlight the parts of the text that contain the main ideas	
Step 2: Write out a list of the main ideas	• Australia has a food waste problem. • Wasting food can lead to climate change. • The home is a large source of food waste. • Small changes can make a big difference. • Changes can be grouped into planning for shopping, shopping, storing food at home, cooking and eating. • The biggest barriers are mental. • Three top behaviours are planning ahead, having a shelf for food to use up and cooking the right amount. • A weekly 'use-it-up meal' is the most effective. • Advanced techniques include a weekly food audit, a shopping list and a meal plan. • Less effective methods include preserving food, making stock and shopping at specialist stores. • Australia has signed up to the UN Sustainable Development Goals and should be trying to halve food waste. • Australia can stop throwing out food and everyone should play a part.
Step 3: Combine any similar ideas together	Australia has a food problem + the home is a source of waste + everyone should play a part. The biggest barriers are mental + small changes can make a big difference + changes can be grouped into planning for shopping, shopping, storing food at home, cooking and eating. Three top behaviours are planning ahead, having a shelf for food to use up and cooking the right amount + a weekly 'use-it-up meal' is the most effective.
Step 4: Organise your list of ideas into order of importance, with the most important ideas at the top of the list	1. Australia has a food waste problem, especially with home food waste and everyone should play a part. 2. Food waste can contribute to climate change. 3. Australia has signed up to the UN Sustainable Goals and should be trying to halve food waste. 4. The biggest barriers are mental, but small changes like planning meals, shopping habits, food storage and how we cook and eat can make a big difference. 5. Behaviours include planning ahead, having a shelf for food to use up, cooking the right amount and a weekly 'use-it-up meal' is the most effective. 6. Advanced techniques include a weekly food audit, a shopping list and a meal plan.
Step 5: Write your summary as a paragraph. The paragraph should contain the most important information from the text	Australia has a food waste problem, especially at home, and everyone should play a part in reducing food waste. Food waste can contribute to climate change, but Australia has signed up to the UN Sustainable Goals and should be trying to halve food waste. The biggest barriers are mental, but small changes like planning meals, shopping habits, food storage and how we cook and eat can make a big difference. Behaviours that reduce food waste include planning ahead, having a shelf for food to use up and cooking the right amount. A weekly 'use-it-up meal' is the most effective behaviour. People who already have these behaviours can use advanced techniques including a weekly food audit, a shopping list and a meal plan.

Reflect

Note how in the example the student has condensed a fairly long article into a very short paragraph but has retained the language of the original text. This is one of the things that differentiates this activity from a paraphrase, which would be written mostly in the student's own words. Although this is a fairly lengthy process, it encourages students to thoroughly read the text rather than just skimming. Every student will come up with a slightly different summary, based on their own opinion of the key points of the text. Working in pairs on this task makes for very useful discussions about these different opinions.

- How would you use this activity with an even longer text, like a novel? Chapter by chapter? Dividing the book into parts? The whole book?
- Is this activity more suitable for junior students or senior, or would it work with both?
- How could you apply these same techniques to a film or multimodal text?

Extend

Summarising activities can naturally lend themselves to more complex tasks such as paraphrasing and evaluating. Beginning with a summary gives the students something to work with. To extend this activity:

- Combine it with Activity 2: Key Idea Paraphrase and have students writing in their own words.
- Use the summary as the starting point for a discussion of the main arguments in a persuasive text, leading on to a persuasive analysis.
- Use the summary to create a new text such as a blurb or a review.

ACTIVITY 2:
KEY IDEA PARAPHRASE

As explained in the introduction, a paraphrase goes beyond a simple summary, as it requires students to use their own language to present the key information from the text. The Key Idea Paraphrase activity adds some structure to this process, taking some of the guesswork out of the act of paraphrasing. Asking students to paraphrase *without* a supporting structure will often lead to a simplistic summary or restatement in the original language of the text.

A word of caution with this activity: monitor the students' use of a thesaurus. Student writing can all too easily turn into gibberish when every word is replaced by the most complex-sounding synonym, and words should always be used in the right context.

Instructions for teachers

☑ A text to be paraphrased
☑ A thesaurus

1. Read through the text to be summarised, either independently or as a class.
2. Identify the key terms and ideas from the text.
3. Optional: find synonyms for the key terms and ideas.
4. Use the key terms to write a new paragraph.

Instructions for students

1. Read the text and identify the key terms and ideas.
2. Optional: use a thesaurus or your own knowledge to write synonyms for those words.
3. Use your five key terms to write a new paragraph in your own words.

Example

From The Conversation website by Mark Andrejevic, Abdul Karim Obeid, Daniel Angus and Jean Burgess

Facebook ads have enabled discrimination based on gender, race and age. We need to know how 'dark ads' affect Australians

Social media platforms are transforming how online advertising works and, in turn, raising concerns about new forms of discrimination and predatory marketing.

Today the ARC Centre of Excellence for Automated Decision Making and Society (ADM+S) – a multi-university entity led by RMIT – launched the Australian Ad Observatory. This research project will explore how platforms target Australian users with ads.

The goal is to foster a conversation about the need for public transparency in online advertising.

The rise of 'dark ads'

In the mass media era, advertising was (for the most part) public. This meant it was open to scrutiny. When advertisers behaved illegally or irresponsibly, the results were there for many to see.

And the history of advertising is riddled with irresponsible behaviour. We've witnessed tobacco and alcohol companies engage in the predatory targeting of women, underage people and socially disadvantaged communities. We've seen the use of sexist and racist stereotypes. More recently, the circulation of misinformation has become a major concern.

When such practices take place in the open, they can be responded to by media watchdogs, citizens and regulators. On the other hand, the rise of online advertising – which is tailored to individuals and delivered on personal devices – reduces public accountability.

These so-called "dark ads" are visible only to the targeted user. They are hard to track, since an ad may only appear a few times before disappearing. Also, the user doesn't know whether the ads they see are being shown to others, or whether they're being singled-out based on their identity data.

Key terms/ideas:

1. Social media platforms
2. Targeting Australian users
3. 'Dark ads'
4. Hard to track
5. Use identity data

Paraphrase:

'Dark ads' aimed at Australian social media users are dangerous because they are difficult to trace.

Reflect

In the example above, note how the student has chosen to focus on one aspect of the text: the difficulty in tracking 'dark ads'. They could just have easily highlighted the "circulation of misleading information", or the tailoring of online ads in their key ideas, but for this activity the important thing is to let the students make their own meaning.

- Comparing this to Activity 1, what is the difference between summary and paraphrase?
- Why is paraphrasing an important skill?
- Could this activity be used with a longer text, such as a feature article or a fiction novel?

Extend

In the example above, the student's response could be used as part of the introduction to an essay. You could also extend this activity by:

- Comparing and discussing students' different interpretations of the text
- Exploring how to extend the paraphrase into a longer text response, for example, by finding supporting evidence from the text

ACTIVITY 3:
10 WORDS OR LESS

This activity provides an excellent basis for a short summary text such as a blog or can be used to prompt a longer piece of writing, such as by condensing the meaning of a text and then reusing that as the basis for a new text or adaptation. Getting students to summarise in 10 words or less requires them to be succinct and accurate with their language.

Instructions for teachers

☑ A text to be summarised

1. Read through the text to be summarised, either independently or as a class.
2. Students must then identify the key ideas from the text and make a note of them.
3. Using these key ideas, students must write a single sentence of 10 words or less summarising the key ideas of the text.

Instructions for students

1. Read through the text to be summarised, either independently or as a class.
2. Identify the key ideas from the text and make a note of them.
3. Write a single sentence of 10 words or less summarising the key ideas of the text.

Example

Students' summary of *Pride and Prejudice by* Jane Austen.

Student 1: Lizzie hates Darcy. Lizzie loves Darcy. They get married.

Student 2: Characters overcome pride and prejudice to fall in love.

Student 3: Society expects lots but people still choose their own path.

Student 4: Two people hate each other then they love each other.

Student 5: In the end, love beats pride and prejudice.

Reflect

Note the varied responses from these students. Some, like 1 and 4, have focused on a summary of plot – Lizzie and Darcy don't like each other at the beginning, and by the end they are married. These also convey that perhaps the students' understandings of the characters are a little shallow (though that's hard to tell in 10 words!). Responses 2 and 5 both focus on how love overcomes pride and prejudice, and response 3 focuses on a more thematic/values-based summary of societal expectations. In their own ways, all of these 10-word summaries are accurate.

♦ The example is taken from an activity based on a long and complex novel. What are the advantages and disadvantages of using a text like this for this activity?
♦ How could you add further instruction to this task to focus it, for example, on a summary of key themes, ideas, moments or characters?
♦ How would this activity work with nonfiction?

Extend

Although it will take students some time to edit their summary back to 10 words or less, this is still a quick activity, making it ideal at the start of the lesson. It can then be extended by:

- Comparing the students' 10-word summaries in a class discussion, and creating a class summary
- Using the 10-word summary as the centre of a mind-mapping activity on the broader text, getting students to identify the aspects of the text that led them to their summary
- Using the 10-word summary as a prompt or stimulus for a longer piece of writing

ACTIVITY 4: ELEVATOR PITCH

In this activity students need to 'sell' the main idea of the text. This blends summarising with persuasive techniques and gets students to think about the main problem in a text, and how the author attempts to address the problem. As such, it's a perfect activity for analysing opinion pieces, speeches and other texts with a clear argument. The pitch component of the activity is based on a 'Gaddie pitch' – a type of elevator pitch commonly used in business proposals.

Instructions for teachers

☑ Text to be summarised and 'pitched'
☑ A copy of the sentence starters for the Gaddie pitch

1. Read the text as a class, in small groups or individually.
2. Highlight and annotate the main ideas in the text and the evidence used to support those ideas. Students should identify the overall contention and the way the author presents their argument or solution.
3. Walk students through the process of the Gaddie pitch. In the first sentence, students must outline the problem or issue the text deals with. Students must complete the sentence stem: *You know how... <problem>*
4. Explain the second part of the pitch. Students must discuss how the author presents an argument or solution to the problem. Students must complete the sentence stem: *Well, <author> suggests/ states/claims...*
5. Explain the final step of the pitch. Students must summarise the evidence/supporting arguments used to back up the author's contention. Students must complete the sentence stem: *In fact... <evidence used to back up the argument>*

Instructions for students

1. Read the text you need to summarise and highlight the key ideas and evidence used to support the ideas.
2. Complete the Gaddie pitch template, beginning with the sentence starter: *You know how...* and identifying the problem/issue being discussed.
3. Complete the second sentence starter: *Well, <author's name> suggests/states/claims...<main argument>*
4. Complete the third sentence starter: *In fact...<summary of evidence/ supporting arguments from the text>*

Example

Students' elevator pitch of a text

You know how... Microplastics in the ocean contribute to animal health issues?

Well, Aubrey Rosenthorpe **suggests...** that if we all stop using bath and shower products containing microplastics now, we might get on top of the problem by 2025.

In fact... Research has shown that over 25% of microplastics in the ocean come from bath and shower products. There are many alternatives available, and not all of them are expensive. Experience has shown that consumer demand can change business practice, so if consumers move away from products with microplastics, companies will stop manufacturing them.

Reflect

This activity works very well with students who are already familiar with methods of summarising. The third part – *In fact...* – relies on students being able to accurately summarise the main supporting arguments and/or evidence. The ability to articulate an author's contention is also a summarising activity, as it requires paraphrasing the main point of the text being studied.

- Could this 'elevator pitch' be used with fiction texts as well as nonfiction/persuasive? What would the students be pitching?
- How could you apply these skills to other forms of text, such as multimodal, video, visual?

Extend

Many forms of expository writing in schools rely on students identifying an author's contention and how they support their arguments. This activity lends itself to both planning a full response and writing an introduction to an analysis of argument. You could also:

- Present the elevator pitches orally in groups or as a class, as if they were real pitches for a product/solution.
- Get students to write their own elevator pitches as the basis for a piece of original writing.
- Use the arguments and evidence identified in the *In fact...* section as the basis of a group or class discussion or debate.

CHAPTER 6

STRATEGY 6: SYNTHESISING

The word 'synthesis' has its origins in Greek and means to 'bring together'. Compare this with another word common to the English classroom: analysis. 'Analysis' comes from *analusis*, which means 'to loosen'. So, when we ask students to analyse, we are asking them to break a text into its component parts – to 'loosen' the text into units of meaning, symbols and ideas. When we ask students to synthesise, on the other hand, we are asking them to bring together all of these disparate points into a new whole.

Synthesis is a higher-order thinking skill and requires both a comprehensive knowledge of the text or texts being studied, and the ability to step back and see the bigger picture. It is a Strategy that unites the other five, bringing together all of the skills used throughout this book so far. Here's how synthesis relates to the other Strategies:

Making Connections: Students synthesise by connecting new knowledge to that which they already know. Being able to make connections to self, other texts and the world allows students to better process and synthesise new knowledge.

Visualising: Synthesis involves hearing the 'inner voice' and relating the text to what a reader pictures in their mind.

Questioning: In order to synthesise from multiple sources of information, or from points across a single text, good readers frame intelligent questions around the text. Seeking the answers to these questions is part of the process of synthesis.

Inferring: Inference means 'reading between the lines'. In order to infer, readers must be able to pull together many different 'clues' from all over the text, including the actions and dialogue of characters, the description of setting, the nuance of symbolism and figurative language, and the author's context.

Summarising: Summarising is often a necessary precursor to synthesising. Before students can synthesise information from a complex text or a range of texts, it is useful to first summarise the key points.

Synthesising is typically an 'end-point' activity. In many ways, the act of writing an essay response itself is an act of synthesis. It asks the reader to step back, to consider the text from multiple angles and, in some cases, to respond to a given prompt. In order for a student to do all of these things, they must be able to identify and synthesise the relevant points from across the text(s).

Finally, synthesising is a Strategy that results in something greater than the sum of its parts. A reader who can synthesise ideas from texts can unlock new and exciting understandings, putting the pieces together to form something new and unique. The activities in this final Strategy are particularly well suited to the end of a unit of work, just before – or, in some cases, in place of – a final assessment piece.

ACTIVITY 1: MEGA MAP

The Mega Map is the culmination of many hours of study. It allows students to pull together all of the separate ideas gleaned from the text over a course of study, and to visualise new links between existing ideas. Importantly, the Mega Map is more than just a revision tool. Students are not simply reorganising or reviewing what they have learned; they are developing a new and deeper awareness about how the parts of the text contribute to the whole.

Instructions for teachers

☑ The text being studied
☑ Other pieces of work completed on the text, such as text walks, visualising activities, questions and prompts
☑ A3 paper, butcher's paper or a digital mind-mapping application

1. Begin by giving time for students to organise all of the work they have completed on the text so far. For example, students might review their Text Files (see Activity 4), lay out physical copies of text walks completed in class or skim through their annotated copies of the text.
2. Model a mind-mapping process that has the text at the centre, and then various bubbles surrounding it. Alternatively, students could connect their existing pieces together by pinning them to a noticeboard or sticking to a whiteboard (see example). These could be:
   a. Characterisation
   b. Narrative structure
   c. Language
   d. Imagery and figurative language
   e. Symbolism
   f. Themes, issues and ideas

g. Author's values

h. Context

i. Key quotes

3. Begin with a class discussion, calling on individual students to add to the modelled mind map. Once students have contributed to the class mind map, provide time for them to create their own.

4. Interrupt the mind-mapping process to model drawing links between different 'bubbles', for example, connecting something in *characterisation* with a related idea in *symbols* or *themes*. Along the connecting lines, write a brief explanation of the link.

5. Provide the students with more time to add to their Mega Maps.

Instructions for students

This mind-mapping activity will bring together as many of the ideas from your study as possible. You will create a mind map that has information on many different elements of the text, such as:

Characterisation; narrative structure; language; imagery and figurative language; symbolism; themes, issues and ideas; author's values; context; and key quotes.

You will also need to draw connections between these ideas, and explain the connections.

Example

Example of students' Mega Map for *Frankenstein* by Mary Shelley

Reflect

This activity can take a *long* time, so it's best to plan ahead. Often, activities like this get left to the last minute, such as during end-of-the-year revision time. Although there is a logic in using mind mapping as a revision aid, planning to devote extra time to an activity like this can lead to big rewards. All readers need time to process the information they have encountered, whether over a full course of study or immediately at the end of a short text.

- How long do you think your class(es) would take to do this activity justice? What can you do to plan for that time?
- What collaborative possibilities exist for this activity? What aspects would work better as a group task, and what suits individual work?

- What would be the value in continuing and completing the class Mega Map used to model the early stages of the process?

Extend

Like the Text File in Activity 4, this activity can be used as a form of assessment itself. It could also be the basis of a series of responses, or extended in other ways:

- Get students to use their Mega Maps to generate exam-style topics of their own.
- Digitise Mega Maps, and create a shared document that links different students' work together.
- Add an audio-visual element to the Mega Maps. Once students have completed their maps, have them record short audio or video files explaining some of the key aspects. These can also be embedded directly into digital versions of the Mega Maps.

ACTIVITY 2: STRATEGY HUB

The Strategy Hub is a graphic organiser that pulls together the key information from the students' other activities over the course of study. As covered in the introduction, synthesising is a higher-order skill that can leverage off all of the other Strategies. This activity highlights that interconnectedness and puts all of the key information onto one page to make it easier to process.

Instructions for teachers

☑ A text that has been studied
☑ Completed activities and tasks from over the course of study, preferably from each of the other five areas
☑ An A3 copy of the Strategy Hub template, a digital copy or blank paper for the students to copy the template onto

1. Begin by allowing students time to organise their notes and resources from previous activities. They should organise their notes by Strategy to make it easier to transfer the key ideas.
2. Model at least one of the sections of the Hub. The intent is to take a few key ideas in each area and transfer them to the Hub, for example, focusing on the most important text-to-text, self and world connections from the Making Connections Strategy.
3. Allow students time to complete their own Strategy Hubs.
4. The final section to be filled in should have the synthesising section at the centre. In this section, students should write a short statement about the text that they feel encapsulates the most important message or meaning.

Instructions for students

This synthesising activity will need you to find the key ideas from each of the other Strategies. The other Strategies are:

Making Connections   Visualising
Questioning   Inferring and Summarising

Begin by organising your notes on the text into Strategies.

Transfer the key ideas and things you have learned from each Strategy to the relevant part of the Hub.

Finally, write a statement at the centre of the Hub that you think clearly states the meaning or message of the text.

Example

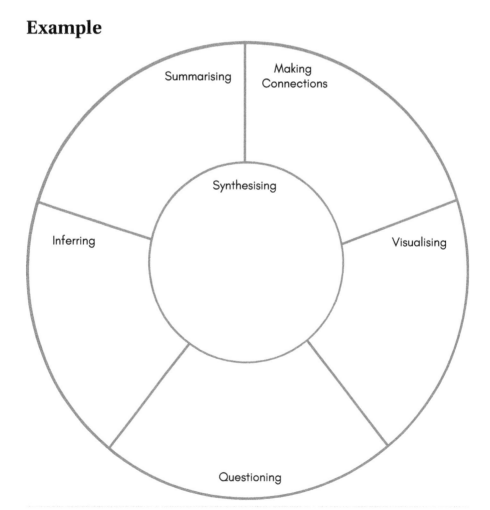

From *Lilith's Brood* by Octavia E Butler

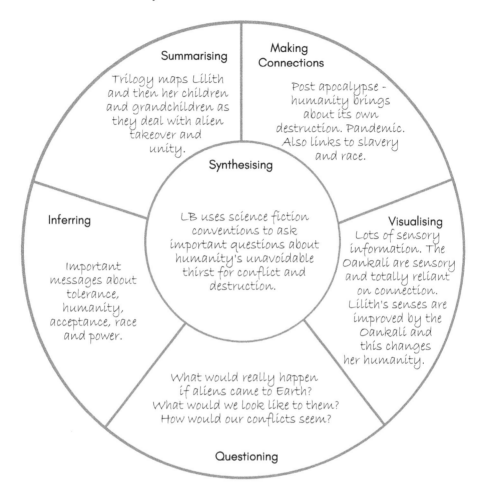

Summarising

Trilogy maps Lilith and then her children and grandchildren as they deal with alien takeover and unity.

Making Connections

Post apocalypse - humanity brings about its own destruction. Pandemic. Also links to slavery and race.

Synthesising

LB uses science fiction conventions to ask important questions about humanity's unavoidable thirst for conflict and destruction.

Inferring

Important messages about tolerance, humanity, acceptance, race and power.

Visualising

Lots of sensory information. The Oankali are sensory and totally reliant on connection. Lilith's senses are improved by the Oankali and this changes her humanity.

Questioning

What would really happen if aliens came to Earth? What would we look like to them? How would our conflicts seem?

Reflect

Getting students to process and condense their notes after a full unit of study can be daunting but offers a very effective way of synthesising the main points from even very complex texts like the one given in the example. In a condensed form, this activity could be carried out in a shorter unit of study by setting one task from each of the other five Strategies, and then using the Hub as a final task.

◆ What do students gain from revisiting earlier tasks in this manner?
◆ What is the purpose or utility of the final synthesising statement at the centre of the Hub?

- How could this activity be used with shorter, simpler texts, but remain effective?

Extend

As mentioned above, the Strategy Hub is another end-of-unit activity, meaning it can be used itself as a form of summative assessment. It could also lead to:

- Using the synthesising comment as the basis for an analytical response
- Connecting this activity to Activity 1: Mega Maps, and using each of the Strategies as the bubbles of the mind map
- A structured discussion either as a class or in groups of six, where each student/group of students is responsible for speaking about their specific Strategy

ACTIVITY 3: SYNTHESISING MOOD BOARD

A mood board uses a collage of words, images, colours and textures to communicate design ideas, a vision or a concept. In the design world, they are commonly used by people in the creative industries to express a new idea. In this activity, students will create a mood board based on their observations from the text they have studied, drawing on multimodal resources to create a board that is both visually inspiring and captures some of the essence of the text.

Instructions for teachers

☑ A text that has been studied
☑ Physical resources for the mood board, such as A3 paper, butcher's paper, magazines, newspapers, coloured paper OR
☑ Digital apps and technologies, such as Canva, Google Slides or PowerPoint

1. It may be useful to begin this activity with some class brainstorming of key concepts, ideas, themes, issues, symbols and so on from the studied text. It could also be useful to complete one of the other synthesising activities or review the Text File (see Activity 4). Students should be prepared to identify useful materials to use on their mood boards, and not spend too much time searching for pictures, colours, text etc.
2. Allow students some time to search online for examples of mood boards, to familiarise them with the concept and style.
3. Provide students with the materials and time to construct the mood board. These may be hard copy or digital. Encourage students to identify materials representative of aspects of the text, for example:
   a. Key ideas from the other five reading Strategies:

Making Connections	Visualising
Questioning	Inferring and Summarising

   b. Themes, issues, ideas and values

c. Symbolism, style and language

d. Characterisation and narrative

Instructions for students

In this activity, you will construct a 'mood board' that pulls together everything you have learned about the text.

1. Search online for a few examples of mood boards. Look at how the designers use layers of images, text, colours and textures.
2. Find materials that represent different aspects of the text, for example:
   a. Key ideas from the other five reading Strategies:

   Making Connections   Visualising

   Questioning   Inferring and Summarising
   b. Themes, issues, ideas and values
   c. Symbolism, style and language
   d. Characterisation and narrative
3. Create your mood board!

Example

Example mood board for *Wonder* by RJ Palacio

Reflect

This is a great activity to end a unit. It is fun and creative, but still requires students to think deeply about the text they have studied. It can also lead to some great discussions around the choices students have made in constructing their boards. Completing this activity with physical resources can be more time consuming, but there is the added bonus of students engaging on a more tactile level with the text. Digital mood boards have the advantage of taking less time and preparation, and they can also include audio/visual materials like sound and video.

- Where does the academic rigour of this activity come from? How can you ensure it is seen as more than just 'making a collage'?
- Could you target the different elements and have students working on specific mood boards, for example, one student or group working on characterisation, another on themes, issues, ideas and values? What are the advantages and disadvantages of this?

Extend

Although a collage would certainly be a non-traditional 'final piece' for an English classroom, the Synthesising Mood Board demonstrates an understanding of the text and an ability to process complex ideas. It may be worth extending the activity by:

- Annotating the mood boards
- Having students produce a written explanation of their board, with details on why they chose certain colours, images and so on
- Using the mood boards as the basis for an open-response essay (with no set topic)

ACTIVITY 4:
THE TEXT FILE

The Text File is both a cumulative and a final product. It evolves over the course of an entire unit of work but is also used beyond the final few pages of the text being studied as a resource, a revision aid and possibly as an assessment itself.

As with many of the activities in this book, I would recommend introducing students to the Text File early, and as soon as they begin studying longer, more complex texts. By the time students reach senior school, they should be so used to the process that the first thing they do upon encountering a new text is to create a Text File for it.

The Text File is a record of all of the interesting points, character observations, notes on themes, issues, ideas and values, key quotes and anything else the reader unearths during their study. It is a document that is constantly evolving and changing to suit the student's individual needs and interests, and allows students both to keep track of their thoughts and to synthesise the great many ideas they will have while reading the text.

Instructions for teachers

☑ A blank document or a template
☑ Notes from any other activity, close reading or annotation of the text being studied

1. Although a synthesising activity, the text file should be created before students have begun studying the text. Have students create their own digital document (a Word doc, a Google Doc or similar) or provide them with a template.

2. As the text is studied in class, encourage students to regularly transfer their notes to their text file into relevant categories. For example, if the students complete a visualising activity that reveals something about a certain character, they should transfer some of these notes to their text file under a 'character' subheading.
3. Create new subheadings as needed, adding to the Text File over the course of study. Occasionally, it is good to offer students time in class to organise, review and update their Text Files.
4. At the end of study, review the Text Files and assess which students have gaps. Address any gaps as necessary.

Instructions for students

Your Text File will become your most useful revision document. Make sure to keep it up to date!

1. Create a new blank document or use the template from the teacher.
2. After you have completed an activity, read a few chapters or discussed ideas in the text, transfer them to your Text File.
3. Every now and again, review your Text File and update it.

Example

Extracts from various students' Text Files for *Frankenstein* by Mary Shelley

NB: It would be impossible to provide a complete example of a Text File in this book – some students at the senior level might have Text Files that stretch to 30 or 40 pages or beyond! These extracts provide an example of different approaches used by different students, to emphasise the fact that the Text File should be a unique document for each reader.

One student uses simple dot-points to record ideas on a theme of nature as they come across them. Another has an Enlightenment versus Romantic Era table, including quotes. A third student writes their own chapter summaries, including quotes and connections to elsewhere in the text.

Example 1: Theme

Nature

- Victor dives into 'natural philosophy'; he is deeply acquainted with nature at the beginning of the text.
- While at university, Frankenstein's lack of contact with the natural world demonstrates the unnaturalness of his task.
- *"Winter, spring and summer passed away during my labours; but I did not watch the blossom or the expanding leaves-before sights which always yielded me supreme delight, so deeply was I engrossed in my occupation..."* – page 57. Perhaps if Frankenstein had been immersed in the countryside around him, he would not have lost sight of his humanity and created his monstrous collection of body parts.
- After the death of William, he heads home in grief but stops at Lake Lausanne where the *"calm and heavenly scene restored him"* – page 76.
- Mary Shelley uses nature to reflect the dreadful events throughout the novel and how disconnection from the natural world of peace and beauty can potentially destroy an individual's humanity and moral perspective.
- Lightning – an important aspect of nature that illuminates the truth throughout the novel – sheds light on Frankenstein's creation.
- Mary Shelley's implication is clear: human beings, weighed down with countless flaws such as vanity and prejudice, pale in comparison to nature's perfection.
- Passion to learn *"the hidden laws of nature"*.
- *"secrets of heaven and earth I desired to learn"* – page 39.
- *"What before was desert and gloomy should now bloom with the most glorious flowers and verdure"* – the weather reflects the monster's mood.
- The monster's behaviour is changed by exposing himself to nature.
- *"Dispelling their sorrow as the sun dissipates the morning mists"* – a new start, cleansing.
- *"Spring advanced rapidly..."* – the monster is in a good mood when it is spring; his emotions are tied to the seasons. The monster is advancing rapidly like spring, becoming less creature and more human.

- *Three different natures*: nature of weather, nature of man (human condition), nature of knowledge (education/knowledge).
- *"My native wood"* – the monster sees nature as his rightful place and home because he is not accepted by humanity, but is accepted by the natural world (animalistic).

Example 2: Context

Enlightenment Era	Romantic Era
Victor Frankenstein defies nature as being natural by creating something so unnatural	The powers of nature are God-like – a religious response to nature
Victor's goal is to progress the natural sciences The monster reads to educate himself and progress his own knowledge and understanding of society	Victor's wonder at alchemy and natural philosophy The monster's reading of old literature reflects an interest in the primitive forms of art
As he seeks revenge against the monster, Victor pursues his own happiness at the expense of the others, which is immoral according to Enlightenment conventions	"imbued with a fervent longing to penetrate the secrets of nature" – capacity for wonder "A child's blindness" – wonder/vision of childhood
Frankenstein is born into the world as a prisoner to his own appearance and lack of education and is therefore not free, which means he is not a human being because according to the Enlightenment era, all human beings are born free and choose how they should best live their lives (liberty)	Shelley is warning ambitious people of the many dangers of disregarding family/limits of nature, which reflects the values of the Romantic era by positioning Mary Shelley the author as a prophetic figure

Example 3: Chapter summary

<u>Volume 1 – Letters I-IV pages 15–32</u>

"Read with ardour the accounts of various voyages" – Walton. Comparable to Frankenstein's reading of alchemy p15
"I bore the disappointment" – Walton relates to how VF handles failure p17.
"Devoted my nights to study" – Walton's behaviour a replica of VF's p17.
"Hopes fluctuate"; *"spirits often depressed"* – Walton similar to VF p17.
"Required to raise spirits of others" – Walton's duty as captain should also have been VF's duty as creator.
Interesting to note Walton's supposed destination is Archangel, a legitimate place, yet there is religious context. An Archangel is supposedly an angel of a higher caste than normal angels, which is evidently what Walton is striving for p17.
"Such a friend would repair the faults" – Walton relates how the creature feels a friend will render him guiltless and change his dastardly way.
VF portrayed same as creature *"Suffering deprived him of understanding"*; *"eyes an expression of wildness"*; *"gnashes his teeth"* p27.
"Restored me to life" – VF to Walton as VF had done to Creature p28.

Reflect

The examples unfortunately cannot do justice to how much information is stored in these students' complete Text Files. The three students who produced these works had experienced Text Files in Years 11 and 12, but did not fully 'get it' until this unit on *Frankenstein*. Once students begin to grasp the power of organising their thoughts and pulling together their disparate notes into one Text File, they unlock a much greater potential for success in their writing on the text.

Students pull ideas into their Text Files from a number of places, transferring across marginalia from their annotated books, copy/pasting digital notes such as those made in a Making Connections activity, or just summarising their thoughts on particular characters, themes, issues, ideas and values.

- What sources of information could go into a Text File?
- What are the advantages of providing a template, for example, a document containing headings for: themes, characters, context, language, values and so on? What are the disadvantages?
- How could you begin to embed Text File ideas earlier, such as in shorter text units in the junior years?

Extend

The Text File can be an end point, a folio of work that demonstrates a student's understanding of the text. If you choose to extend beyond this point, however, the Text File can be used in a number of ways:

- Have students turn their Text File into a deck of cue cards for a structured, purposeful revision aid.
- Use the contents of the Text File to derive student-generated essay prompts.
- Identify gaps and strengths in students' Text Files, and form workshop groups where students help each other.

PART 2

CHAPTER 7

COMBINING STRATEGIES

Once you have experimented with the six Strategies and the activities in part one of this book, it's time to get creative and start thinking of ways to combine and extend. The Strategies are a convenient way of categorising skills related to reading, but in reality, reading is a much more complicated process. The hierarchy presented in part one – beginning with Making Connections and culminating in Synthesising – is a useful framework when you're beginning with the Strategies. This chapter will provide a few suggestions for how the Strategies might be combined in order to link together various skills and ideas.

Making Connections

The Connections activities, centred on the Text Walk, provide a perfect opportunity for experimenting with combinations. Consider:

♦ A Text Walk that requires students to annotate extracts with Questions or Inferences
♦ A text-to-text activity based on a comparison of a written text to a visual counterpart, for example, a film version of a novel. Use a Visualising activity such as a Sensory Scene, which can be applied to both texts
♦ A Connections Map, which links together the Summaries of multiple texts based on a theme or issue, for example, a collection of articles on a media issue, or a collection of thematic short stories and poems

Visualising

The Visualising tasks prompt a full sensory exploration of a text and can be used for a wide variety of text types. These tasks are well suited to working in combination with the Inferring tasks, for example:

♦ Combining the Visualising task Reading in Role with the Inferring task How do they feel? How do you know? by completing the performance followed by the analysis
♦ Using the quotes identified in the Sensory Scenes activity as the basis for the inferential QPCI activity
♦ Getting students to Read Between the Lines before making a Soundscape and having them include their inferences in the written explanation of the latter task.

Questioning

Because the Questioning activities are based around *students* forming their own questions, rather than teachers asking them, they are ideally suited to paring up with a range of other activities, such as:

- Using a Four Questions activity prior to completing any of the Making Connections activities, and having students attempt to answer or address some of their own questions
- Having the students write some Deep Questions as the basis for a Visualising task, for example, by using some of their questions as the basis for a Sensory Scene or a Soundscape
- Using student-generated questions – and their answers – as the basis for a Summary of the text(s) being studied

Inferring

Inferring is a complex skill to develop and to teach. Much of a student's ability to infer comes from their context, including their world view, experience and everything else they have read. This makes Making Connections tasks an ideal 'way in' to inference.

- Before asking students to Read Between the Lines, contextualise the materials being studied with a Context Walk.
- Use Text Walks to reduce the burden on individual students by allowing them to annotate and develop inferences in groups.
- Explore the similarities and differences between key quotes from related texts, combining a Connections Map of various texts with a QPCI activity. Examine how *intertextuality* allows us to build inferences.

Summarising

Rather than treating Summarising activities as an end point, intersperse the activities throughout a unit, and combine them with other Strategies to summarise different aspects of the text(s) being studied, for example:

- Producing a Guided Summary of a class Text Walk
- Completing a 10 Words or Less summary at the end of any other activity, asking students to briefly summarise the content of what they have learned
- Having students construct an Elevator Pitch of their key ideas from any other activity, to try to 'sell' what they have learned to other students

Synthesising

By its very nature, Synthesis is a skill that requires combining other skills and ideas. As well as the Mega Map and Strategy Hub, consider:

- Making a Mood Board of a group of students' works in another activity, for example, a Sensory Scene. Have students compare their scenes and identify overlapping moods and ideas
- Synthesising ideas from *within* the Strategy itself, for example, having a group of students use their Text Files to create a collaborative Mega Map
- Synthesising any of the activities by pulling together the reflections, summaries, written explanations or any other written outcomes into a final response

As you can see, these are just a few examples of how the Strategies can be combined and used to either reinforce one another, or to come up with totally new activities. The more confident you become with the basics of each of the six Strategies, the easier you will find it to invent your own activities that are engaging, purposeful and tailored to your students' needs.

CHAPTER 8

CONSTRUCTING A UNIT OF WORK

There are many ways to build a unit of work around the Strategies. In this chapter, I'll go through two detailed units of work that involve the Strategies, one a more conventional unit, and the other built entirely around the activities in this book.

Depending on your faculty, the degree of autonomy you have over your curriculum and the appetite for change, you might choose to bring the Strategies into your reading units slowly, building the capacity of the teachers through the conscientious use of just a few key activities such as the Text Walk. On the other hand, you might decide that an entire unit is due for an overhaul, and that you can justifiably throw in your lot with all six Strategies at once.

Whichever way you choose to go, it is important to reflect on one of the messages from the introduction: the Strategies are not hierarchical, but there is a logic to the order in which they are approached in this book. I would advise against 'crowbarring' more complex activities, such as those from the Inferring and Synthesising chapters, into existing units.

It would be far better to familiarise students – and the teachers in your team – with some of the more accessible activities to begin with.

The following two examples are for a Year 7 or 8 English unit on Phillip Pullman's *Northern Lights* (or *The Golden Compass* in the US). This excellent text is rich and complex but with characters and a storyline compelling enough to engage reluctant readers. I've used Australian Curriculum standards for consistency, though I would personally refer to the Victorian Curriculum.

Example one: The 'bolt-on'

In this first example, an existing unit on *Northern Lights* has been 'upgraded' with some of the Reading Strategies activities. The eight-week unit originally focused more on comprehension of the text than on the strategies used to decode it, and as such, the focus of the upgrade is on replacing *content* with *skills*.

Importantly, the baby has not been thrown out with the bathwater. Anyone familiar with curriculum design or faculty leadership will know that it is easy to lose staff support when units are changed and redesigned too frequently: teachers like to know that there is a plan to follow, and that it is not going to suddenly change a few months or weeks before the unit begins.

The core of the unit – it's structure around characterisation, setting and theme – remains from the original. The difference is that Reading Strategies have been used explicitly to embed transferrable skills that will help students beyond just the study of this single text.

Original unit of work

Week	Focus	Content/Activities
1	Introduction to text, how authors build tension	Lesson on context and genre. Discussion of opening pages.
2	Establishing setting	Presentation on Oxford. Examples of settings from the text.
3	Characters and characterisation	Character profile: Lyra. Character profile: Pantalaimon.
4	Theme: Love and friendship	Presentation: Love and friendship in *Northern Lights*. Chapter-based comprehension questions – theme of love and friendship.
5	Theme: Growing up	Presentation: Love and friendship in *Northern Lights*. Chapter-based comprehension questions – theme of growing up.
6	Theme: Good and evil	Presentation: Love and friendship in *Northern Lights*. Chapter-based comprehension questions – theme of good and evil.
7	Symbolism and motifs	What are symbols? Eyes, bears and northern lights: Presentation on symbols in *Northern Lights*.
8	Written response	Response to prompt. Choice of three theme-based prompts.

Note how, in the original unit, there are a number of activities focused on specific elements of the text: two of the characters, Lyra and Pantalaimon; specific themes; and symbols and motifs provided by the teacher. There is also a series of lessons on theme, which are reliant on comprehension questions.

The unit in its current form might result in students gaining an understanding of *Northern Lights*. It is unlikely, however, that they will be prepared to transfer that understanding to other texts. For example, a character profile on Lyra will not necessarily lend itself to a high-quality profile on a character in another text. An exploration of a given theme – such as 'growing up' – will not prepare students to identify *theme* in another novel. Didactic units of work such as this will lead towards a narrow skill set focused on a single text. Unfortunately, due to the nature of high-stakes testing in senior English, this is often how set texts are taught.

The following shows how a few simple changes can upgrade this unit.

Upgraded unit of work

Week	Focus	Content/Activities
1	Introduction to text, how authors build tension	Lesson on context and genre using Context Walk. Guided close reading of opening pages.
2	Establishing setting	Sensory Scenes: Extracts with setting detail of Oxford. Discussion: What do you notice about the setting? Presentation on Oxford.
3	Characters and characterisation	Reading in role: Lyra. Fishbowl discussion – how do authors craft their characters? How do they feel? How do you know?: Pantalaimon Venn diagram comparison of two characters.
4	Theme	Four Questions activity. Deep Questions activity. Discussion of the themes identified through questioning activities.
5	Theme	Group work: Identify close reading passages based around a selected theme.
6	Theme	Group-led presentations on various themes from the text.
7	Symbolism and motifs	What are symbols? Read Between the Lines activity using short extracts focused on symbolic use of eyes and bears.
8	Written response	Response to prompt. Choice of three student-generated prompts.

Firstly, the structure of the unit remains the same. It still involves moving through the text systematically and identifying characterisation, setting, theme and symbols. Some of the activities, particularly those that require explicit instruction such as *What are symbols* and the *Presentation on Oxford* remain from the original.

Note, however, how the Oxford presentation has been moved to after the Sensory Scenes activity. This is a key aspect of the Reading Strategies – encourage students to form their own opinions of the text before shaping their perspectives.

The work on characterisation has also shifted from a simple profile to a much more robust discussion of the craft of writing, and also includes a comparative task between the two characters. Both the Reading in Role and fishbowl discussion encourage students to engage with characters in a more sophisticated manner than the profile, and the How do they feel? How do you know? activity encourages a deeper reading of the text.

The most dramatic change comes in the lessons on theme. Rather than the teacher presenting information on the class about pre-selected themes, Questioning activities are used to generate a student list. There may be some deviation from the original themes of love and friendship, growing up, and good and evil – this is to be expected, and can often lead to rich and interesting discussions. Once themes have been identified by students, they are then developed in discussions and activities over the next few lessons. Ultimately, these themes are used to generate the prompts that students will write their responses to.

Key points from the upgraded unit:
◆ The structure of the unit remains the same, as does the central text
◆ Some explicit instruction remains from the original unit
◆ Activities are flipped to prioritise the student perspective first
◆ Themes are identified through questioning and discussion
◆ Students write their own prompts

Example two: The 'overhaul"

Sometimes, a unit needs a significant overhaul. It may be the case that the text is engaging and interesting for students, but the teaching methods in the unit are dry and too teacher-led. The outcome might be unsuitable, for example, requiring extensive written responses from students who are unprepared for longer essays. Or it might simply be a bit boring, both for the teacher and the students.

There are often times when a unit of work would be better off started again than upgraded. Before getting rid of a quality text, it is worth considering a total restructure around the Reading Strategies, shifting the focus of the unit away from character, setting and theme, and towards a systematic exploration of the Strategies.

Refer back to the original *Northern Lights* unit on page 139 and then review the following 'Reading Strategies Folio' unit.

Reading Strategies Folio unit

Week	Focus	Content/Activities
1	Introduction to the Reading Strategies	Overview of the six Reading Strategies, introduction to the folio assessment, introduction to text and genre. Creation of blank Text File.
2	Making Connections	Context walk. Text Walk on opening passages with guided annotation on text-to-text, self and world connections.
3	Visualising	Line-by-Line visualisation: Select key moments from the text for study. Reading in Role: Select key moments from the text for study. Upgrade Text File.
4	Questioning	Four Questions activity. Deep Questions activity. Discussion of the themes identified through questioning activities.
5	Inferring	QPCI. Meaning Map using themes identified in week 4. Upgrade Text File.
6	Summarising	Guided Summary. 10 Words or Less. Fishbowl discussion of summaries and key ideas/themes/issues from the text.
7	Synthesising	Mega Map. Strategy Hub. Complete Text File.
8	Folio submission	Redrafting, editing, peer editing and submission of folio (and/or Text File).

The unit has been entirely restructured around the six Reading Strategies. Some of the original ideas – such as the use of Questioning to identify key themes – remain from the upgraded first unit. Overall, however, the unit has moved away from a discussion of *Northern Lights* and towards a skills-based unit centred on the Strategies. In fact, this unit plan could now be applied to any text, with very different results.

For example, the central text of *Northern Lights* could be replaced with a nonfiction biography, or a collection of persuasive articles on an issue, or a multimodal text such as a graphic novel or film. The Strategies will work with any of those text types.

The other important aspect of this overhauled unit is the creation of a Strategies Folio and a Text File in place of the original written assessment. The following chapter will go into the folio assessment in detail, and the Text File is covered in Chapter 6. Collecting assessment over the course of the unit takes the pressure off the students and allows them some autonomy. They can choose their most successful pieces from each Strategy to submit for assessment, including alternatives to longer, written outcomes such as the Mega Map and their annotations from Text Walks and Context Walks.

Key points from the overhauled unit:
- Because the unit is no longer structured around character, setting and theme, it can be applied to a range of text types.
- Assessment has shifted from an 'end product' to a folio, and from a long, written response to a collection of shorter, focused responses.
- Each of the six Strategies is introduced and taught explicitly, and reinforced through multiple activities.

Embedding the Reading Strategies into your curriculum

Chapter 11 will discuss this in more detail, but the 'overhauled' version of this unit serves as a good example of one way to begin embedding the Strategies across the English curriculum. Because the unit is deliberately skills based and not dependent on a certain text, it can be reused across different year levels, or even from one term or semester to the next, using different texts to reinforce the same skills. Activities can be swapped out, and other skill-centred learning activities such as those from Ron Ritchhart's *Making Thinking Visible* or Doug Lemov's *Reading Reconsidered* can be used in their place.

With staff who are unfamiliar with the Reading Strategies, I would suggest reviewing your existing units and looking for opportunities for upgrading rather than overhauling. Once staff becomes familiar with the activities – either by trialling them in the classroom or through Professional Learning and faculty meetings – then discussions can be held around creating Strategy folio units.

CHAPTER 9

FOLIO-BASED ASSESSMENT

Portfolios offer an excellent way to assess student learning without relying on the sometimes-overwhelming end-of-unit test or essay. They can also offer a greater degree of student autonomy when students are permitted to select which items to submit as part of their portfolio.

In the previous chapter, the 'overhauled' unit plan centred on a folio containing evidence of all six Reading Strategies. This chapter will go into more detail on possible ways of assessing such a folio of work.

Assessing folios

One of the pitfalls of folio-based assessment is that it can result in an overwhelming volume of work if not handled correctly. Although students submit a complete folio at the end of the unit, each piece should have been sighted by the teacher, have received feedback and been edited by the student prior to the final submission. This means that assessing the final submission should take less time than marking a class set of essays or creative pieces – when done well, most of the assessment and feedback is complete long before the end of the unit.

There are several ways to approach giving feedback on folio items. Sometimes, internal processes around marking and assessment might get in the way. For example, your school may have a policy that dictates that all assessments must receive a percentage grade, a letter grade or another numerical grade. Do the components of the folio contribute to this final letter or number equally? Is a Text Walk 'worth' as much as a Mega Map? And what if one student elects to submit a multimodal piece – one of the posters, for example, or the Soundscape – and another submits a longer written piece?

The key to assessing folios is to use developmental or formative rubrics, which are based on the application of the Strategies. Rather than assessing the knowledge of the text, you are assessing the manner in which the student has approached the Strategy. With this in mind, it is perfectly reasonable to assume that a student can submit a complex, sophisticated Mind Map and demonstrate the same – or higher – skills as a student who writes an essay response. The purpose of the developmental rubric is not to just aim for the 'highest' grade, but to accurately assess where a student is, and work with them on what they need to do to move further.

Over the course of the unit, each of the six Strategies can be broken down into a single criterion for the complete rubric. The following rubric shows one example of how you might approach this.

Making Connections	Struggles to connect with the text.	Makes some connections to the text, particularly text-to-self. For example, bases judgements of the text on prior knowledge.	Makes a number of connections to the text, extending beyond just personal connections. For example, is able to discuss connections to other texts, or to events in the real world.	Makes increasingly complex connections to self, world and other texts. Able to explain how these connections enrich the reading of the text.	Makes complex and varied connections to self, world and other texts. Able to explain how these connections enrich the reading of the text.
Visualising	Struggles to visualise the text.	Able to visualise some elements of the text, relying on some support to understand the text first.	Able to visualise a scene by picturing scenes. Identifies important details from the text to help with visualisations.	Able to visualise a scene using specific details from the text to help with the visualisation. Engages the senses.	Able to visualise a scene or scenes from the text, using specific details and cues from the writer to help with the visualisation. Engages the senses, and tries to take the perspective of characters in the text.
Summarising	Struggles to summarise or evaluate the text.	Able to provide basic descriptions of key moments studied in class.	Able to provide summaries of key moments in the text, and to evaluate the importance of those moments.	Selects moments from the text and evaluates their importance. Paraphrases accurately without retelling.	Can select key moments from the text, and evaluates their importance. Is able to paraphrase the text without relying on retelling or describing.
Questioning	Struggles to ask questions beyond searching for word definitions.	Questions are largely searching for definitions, with some beginning to explore the text in more detail.	Asks questions, which shows a growing understanding of text study. Still has questions about definitions, but knows where to look to find answers.	Able to discuss the text in more detail, asking questions that go beyond definitions. Able to answer other students' questions about the text. Knows where to search for answers to increasingly difficult questions.	Able to discuss the text, asking important questions about how the author positions the reader. Able to answer other students' questions and prompt further discussion. Can identify parts of the text that are difficult to understand, and knows how to find answers and support explanations.
Inferring	Struggles to move beyond the 'story level'.	Makes some inferences, showing an increased awareness of how the text is constructed.	Shows an understanding that the text has more than one level, and is able to explain some of the writer's choices.	Makes observations about the text, and can see that the text has multiple layers. Is beginning to explain how the author manipulates language.	Uses an 'inner voice' to help understand what is happening while reading the text. Can see that the text has multiple layers, and is able to explain how the author manipulates language and positions the reader.
Synthesising	Struggles to pull together prior knowledge and new ideas.	Attempts to engage with new ideas, and understands some of _the strategies.	Understands how some of the strategies can build a better understanding of the text. Links to some prior knowledge.	Able to reflect on some of the strategies, and can select where some are more useful than others. Links new knowledge to prior ideas.	Can reflect on all the strategies, identifying where certain strategies are more helpful than others. Is able to link prior knowledge to new ideas. Has developed an enriched understanding of the text over the course.

Breaking down the folio

Rather than presenting the students with the whole rubric, I would suggest addressing the criteria individually as you introduce the Strategies. Begin each new Strategy with an overview of the purpose, for example, explaining how Making Connections allows us to link to other things we have read and seen, and to contextualise what we read. Then, introduce the rubric element:

Struggles to connect with the text.	Makes some connections to the text, particularly text-to-self. For example, bases judgements of the text on prior knowledge.	Makes a number of connections to the text, extending beyond just personal connections. For example, is able to discuss connections to other texts, or to events in the real world.	Makes increasingly complex connections to self, world and other texts. Able to explain how these connections enrich the reading of the text.	Makes complex and varied connections to self, world and other texts. Able to explain how these connections enrich the reading of the text.

Discuss the rubric with your students. Talk about the differences between the descriptors, and how they think they might demonstrate moving from one to another. For example:

Teacher: *If you're working at this level [2], you're making some connections with the text we're reading. You might recognise something similar to another thing you've seen or heard in the past. Maybe you've experienced something similar yourself. Can anyone think of any examples when you have read something in a book, and it has connected with something from your past?*

Or

Teacher: *At level 4, you're linking to things from your own life, other texts and the world. You can also explain why these connections are important – what they mean to you, and to the text. At level 5, these links are 'complex and varied'. What's the difference between the two levels?*

Another way to approach the rubric is to provide models and examples at various levels. Ideally, these will come from your own students.

Building a bank of models

The best way to demonstrate how students can achieve certain levels is to provide models. Discussing models with students allows them to see first-hand what they need to do to achieve a certain level, and to progress through the levels. There are several ways to build up a bank of models.

1. From your own students: These are the best models. Once you have established the Reading Strategies and started to use the activities, you will quickly have access to work that can be saved for future students. Keep a scan or a copy of a couple of high-, medium- and low-range responses from every major task you set. This applies to all of the activities, from the Concept Maps to the longer, written pieces.

2. From online resources: Often, it is possible to find levelled examples of writing online. These will not be specific to the Reading Strategies – it is unlikely that you'll find an example of a completed Strategy Hub or a Mega Map – but you will be able to find examples of essays at various levels, particularly for senior students. Look for examination reports, standardised tests, and even blogs and websites from other English teachers.

3. Write them yourself: Though it can be time-consuming, sometimes it is a good idea to write models yourself, or in a team of teachers working on the same unit. This allows you to experience the activity through the students' eyes and check for any problems that might crop up. Be careful not to 'overwrite' the answers – you'll need to be very conscious of the actual levels of the students you are writing for.

Using the models against criteria

Once you have your models – wherever you got them from – you can now use them to highlight examples of the criteria. You might do this using a 'Think Aloud' while annotating the model. The following two examples demonstrate a level 2 and level 5 example of a Guided Summary for the book *The Dons* by Archimede Fusillo, using the criteria for the Summarising Strategy.

Struggles to summarise or evaluate the text.	Able to provide basic descriptions of key moments studied in class.	Able to provide summaries of key moments in the text, and to evaluate the importance of those moments.	Selects moments from the text and evaluates their importance. Paraphrases accurately without retelling.	Can select key moments from the text, and evaluates their importance. Is able to paraphrase the text without relying on retelling or describing.

Example one:

Step five: Write your summary as a paragraph. The paragraph should contain the most important information from the text.	Paul is angry because he lives with his grandfather and mother, and he is bored. In the end he respects his grandfather more.

Struggles to summarise or evaluate the text.	Able to provide basic descriptions of key moments studied in class.	Able to provide summaries of key moments in the text, and to evaluate the importance of those moments.	Selects moments from the text and evaluates their importance. Paraphrases accurately without retelling.	Can select key moments from the text, and evaluates their importance. Is able to paraphrase the text without relying on retelling or describing.

Teacher's comments: We covered the basics of the storyline in class; at the start, Paul is bored and frustrated, but by the end, he understands his Nonno much more. This student has not identified anything more than the basics of those key parts of the text – they have not *evaluated* how or why those things are important.

Example two:

Step five: Write your summary as a paragraph. The paragraph should contain the most important information from the text.	Paul's Nonno is quite old, and sometimes acts in ways that embarrass Paul. Paul is frustrated with his home life: his father died five years ago and his mother dedicates a lot of her time to looking after Nonno. After learning more about Nonno's life, Paul eventually comes to appreciate and understand him, and learns more about dignity and respect.

Struggles to summarise or evaluate the text.	Able to provide basic descriptions of key moments studied in class.	Able to provide summaries of key moments in the text, and to evaluate the importance of those moments.	Selects moments from the text and evaluates their importance. Paraphrases accurately without retelling.	Can select key moments from the text, and evaluates their importance. Is able to paraphrase the text without relying on retelling or describing.

Teacher's comments: This summary is concise (straight to the point) and identifies the most important aspects of the text without just retelling the story. It also states *why* these points are important, for example, pointing out that coming to understand Nonno also helps Paul to learn about 'dignity and respect'.

.

CHAPTER 10

DEVELOPING AN
ENGLISH CURRICULUM

There is more to an English curriculum than just reading, but being strategic about how often you teach reading, and which texts and Strategies to adopt, can make the rest of the curriculum fall neatly into place. If we begin an English curriculum with reading at centre stage, then we can also avoid one of the biggest pitfalls of curriculum planning: teaching to the exam.

In Victoria, where I'm based, the end of Year 12 examination dominates the English curriculum. I've spoken to teachers in different states and territories, and different countries including the US and UK, who say the same thing: we teach the skills required by the exam because we have to. Where standardised tests come into play – such as the SATs in the US, or NAPLAN in Australia – there is an extra layer of complexity. Standardised tests do not lend themselves to the kind of complex, thoughtful discussions of text outlined in this book. Reading is generally reduced to multiple choice, and writing is so structured that it can be assessed by an algorithm – though luckily that proposal was eventually scrapped. In an education system geared towards these kinds of high-stakes exams and assessments, it can be difficult to imagine a curriculum that doesn't point towards the end product, whether it's a three-hour written exam, or a 45-minute multiple choice.

But teaching English is not about the examination. It's about exploring the many wonderful and complex facets of great texts. It's about encouraging critical thinking, media literacy, argument and debate. Teaching English should offer an opportunity for every student to access increasingly complex texts, with ideas that will take them outside themselves, and encourage empathy and deep thought. All of that starts with reading.

Here's a typical example of a Year 7-10 curriculum. It is based on the state and country I work in, as that's the frame of reference I am most familiar with. However, it is probably applicable to wherever you work – a case in point for the formulaic nature of teaching to the exam.

Year Level	Term 1	Term 2	Term 3	Term 4
7	Persuasive writing/ narrative writing	Reading/ literacy revision NAPLAN	Creative writing	Text study Debates
8	Creative writing	Film study	Text study	Persuasive writing
9	Persuasive writing/ narrative writing	Reading/ literacy revision NAPLAN	Theme unit	Text study
10	Analytical writing	Comparative writing	Analytical writing	Persuasive writing/orals

Notes on the traditional curriculum

- Look at how the first two terms of Years 7 and 9 are dominated by persuasive writing and narrative writing, and the revision of literacy and reading skills – the areas assessed by Australia's standardised NAPLAN test. The 'literacy' being revised in these contexts includes spelling, punctuation and grammar. There are likely NAPLAN practice exams held at the end of Term 1, or the start of Term 2 (or both).
- By Year 10, the curriculum is finished with NAPLAN and sets its sights on higher things – in this case, the VCE exam. Creative writing and film study, as well as some of the oral units, start to take a back seat to analytical writing, persuasive and comparative (the three modes currently assessed in the exam).
- There is a game attempt at a 'thematic' unit in Year 9, but it is not repeated. This one-shot type of unit is common in schools, particularly where an individual teacher or small group is keen to try something new – but only within the safe confines of Year 7-9 before the serious work of Year 12 preparation kicks in.

Problems with the traditional curriculum

The most obvious issue with this form of English curriculum is that it limits the experience to a narrowly defined set of text types and forms, largely centred on the NAPLAN writing modes of persuasive and narrative, and then the senior school analytical and persuasive. This pushes creative writing down the agenda by Year 10 and relegates speaking and listening tasks to the bottom of the pile.

When reading is taught, it is generally connected to a 'set text' – a whole-class novel, collection of short stories, piece of nonfiction, or perhaps poetry or film. This often degrades into 'teaching the text'. There is little time to focus on the skills or strategies involved in reading, because at the end of the day, *all* of these assessments are ultimately tilted towards the three-hour written exam at the end of senior school.

The alternative

In order to shift away from this traditional curriculum structure, you must first be willing to put aside the emphasis on standardised tests and high-stakes examinations. This is the greatest challenge for any head of department, assistant principal or principal. Because this is a book on Reading Strategies, and not a political discourse (although talking about reading *is* political), I'd encourage you to do your own research into *why* to shift focus away from these kinds of assessments.

Instead, here is an example of the kinds of units you might include in restructuring a curriculum. I've tried to make the titles of the units self-explanatory, and they serve more as prompts for ideas than examples of developed units. I deliberately avoid a term-by-term approach because some of these units might be more suited to two- or three-week sprints, and others longer and more project based. Some might work well as cross-curricular units, and others as extracurricular or extensions.

The key is to find a balance of units, and to try to provide a balance of modes, forms, issues and texts so that all students can access a rich and engaging curriculum.

Year 7

- Digital identity: Curating, creating and maintaining a safe digital identity
- Reading Strategies unit: Choose your own text
- Personal writing: Reflection, journaling and memoirs
- Media literacy: Understanding how social media influences us
- Digital texts: Exploring video game narratives
- The Hero Journey: Exploration of texts that follow the hero journey, including examples of different text types
- Introduction to public speaking and debating

Year 8

- Digital texts: Exploring First Nations' voices through video games and animation (Bacalja & Clark, 2021)
- Thematic unit: UN Sustainability Goals; developing an app to persuade, inform and advise
- Writing for others: Blogs, articles and creative nonfiction
- Presenting: Developing presentations, videos and vlogs
- Media literacy: Understanding bias
- Reading Strategies unit: Thematic short stories
- Introducing Classics: Study of classic short stories

Year 9

- Constructing a Text File: Class set text study
- Building inference skills: Collection of poetry with activities focused on inference
- Digital texts: Constructing websites for specific audiences
- Analysing media texts: Opinion pieces and editorials
- Imaginative writing: Speculative fiction
- Debating and argument

Year 10

- Asking questions and interrogating texts: Mixture of fiction and nonfiction used to focus on Questioning strategies
- Analytical writing: Answering the big questions about texts
- Imaginative writing: Responding to world events
- Digital texts: Long-form journalism and online feature articles
- Media literacy: Understanding the big picture – how the media sets agendas
- Public speaking: ideas pitchfest

Notes on these suggestions

This isn't an extensive list of units that can be taught in English, but it is indicative of some of the great units of work I've seen being taught across many schools in Australia. The progression through Year 7 to 10 focuses on building the students' skill sets very deliberately. Whereas a traditional curriculum requires Year 7s to immediately write in both persuasive and narrative modes (and for some schools even, analytical), these units build gradually from personal, reflective writing up to analytical in Year 10. Students will still be prepared for senior school English, but without the unnecessary burden of beginning analytical writing before they are fully prepared.

From a teaching point of view, it is very refreshing to offer students in Years 7 and 8 more opportunities to explore and develop their own 'voice' as opposed to filling their heads with limiting structures like TEEL or a list of 'key quotes' from a class text.

There is also a balance of digital texts, including video games (Bacalja & Clark, 2021), reading, writing, media literacy, and speaking and listening. All of these various forms of literacy are important for a student preparing to navigate a world filled with complex texts, many of which are designed to persuade and mislead. The traditional approach – relying on NAPLAN and senior school-style persuasive texts – is unfortunately divorced from the real world.

And yet, the skills learned in addressing real critical media literacy are applicable to those standardised and high-stakes exams. What works for NAPLAN does not work in the real world, but what works in the real world *does* work for NAPLAN. This is the most important part of creating a diverse and engaging English curriculum. I have seen first-hand how changing the teaching practice to focus on reading before writing, and on putting the student's experience of the text at centre stage, improves results in senior school English.

CHAPTER 11

READING ACROSS
THE CURRICULUM

To discuss a topic as complex as whole-school literacy would take an entire book. In our own school, we have been developing ways of implementing Disciplinary Literacy strategies, particularly across English, Humanities and Science. Getting staff buy-in, finding resources and training teachers who may not be familiar with literacy practices presents a number of roadblocks on the way to a successful whole-school literacy program.

This chapter will focus on just a few examples of how to use the Reading Strategies across other curriculum areas. It is not intended to be a complete guide to whole-school literacy, but it should serve as an interesting conversation starter across subject areas. Whether you are an English teacher, a head of English, a Literacy coordinator or a teacher of a domain other than English, you should find some common ground here to begin the discussion of literacy in your area.

One method we have found successful in implementing whole-school literacy practices is to adapt the Reading Strategies to suit content from different domains. Because they are skills based, the activities in this book can be used with any text, and that means texts outside of English. Once you have read the following examples, discuss them with a member of the relevant faculty and see if they're willing to experiment. Literacy continues to be a complex problem for every subject teacher; providing clear and practical ways of improving students' literacy usually appeals to any teacher.

MAKING CONNECTIONS

The Text Walk in Science

The Text Walk is an excellent activity that can be adopted in any subject area with complex texts that can be broken into extracts. Having the text broken down provides opportunities for deeper discussion of aspects such as purpose, style, conventions and audience.

In this example, the Text Walk is applied to a scientific journal – a genre with its own formula and conventions that must be learned early on. The extracts come from Science Journals for Kids, an excellent online resource that contains many journal articles in a format that will prepare science students for success.

The Text Walk can be structured by asking students to annotate for the purpose of each section, and any specific language or vocabulary used. This could then be followed up with a discussion of each section of the journal article: the abstract, the introduction, the results and so on.

Example

Extracts from www.sciencejournalforkids.org/wp-content/
uploads/2021/09/copper_article.pdf (T Bui, Kang & Urban, 2021)

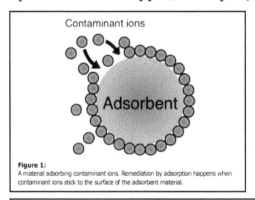

Figure 1:
A material adsorbing contaminant ions. Remediation by adsorption happens when contaminant ions stick to the surface of the adsorbent material.

Abstract

When you think of a glass of water, what words come to mind? Clean? Safe? Refreshing? Unfortunately, those words don't describe most of the drinking water in the world. According to the World Health Organization, 1 in 3 people on Earth don't have access to safe drinking water. Children in some parts of Africa, for example, may need to walk for miles to get access to a bottle of drinking water. No matter where you live, people need clean water. Think about it. We need water for drinking, cooking, bathing, handwashing, and growing food. We need water to survive.

Results

We placed both ZIOS and ZIF-8 in a solution with initial copper ion levels of 425 parts per million (ppm). After 30 minutes, ZIOS had reduced the copper levels to less than 1.5 ppm, while ZIF-8 had dropped the levels to about 42 ppm. After 75 minutes, the copper concentration in the solution with ZIOS was still less than 1.5 ppm, but the levels for ZIF-8 had increased to 115 ppm.

When we tested these adsorbents in water with lots of ions, ZIOS adsorbed 98% of the copper ions, but ZIF-8 only adsorbed about 53%. ZIOS and ZIF-8 also lowered the iron and nickel levels. ZIOS removed more iron and nickel than ZIF-8 (Fig. 3A).

When the pH was low, ZIOS lowered the copper levels, but it did not lower the iron and nickel levels. ZIF-8 had the opposite effect: at low pH, ZIF-8 adsorbed high levels of iron, but not copper (Fig. 3B).

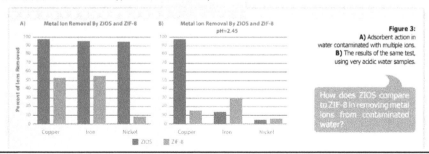

Figure 3:
A) Adsorbent action in water contaminated with multiple ions.
B) The results of the same test, using very acidic water samples.

How does ZIOS compare to ZIF-8 in removing metal ions from contaminated water?

Reflect

Text Walks are by far the most commonly used Reading Strategy activity in my English classroom, but the application across other domains is simple and practical.

◆ How would a Text Walk look for a case study in Health and PE?
◆ What about a visual Text Walk with multiple artworks from the same era, artist or style?
◆ Would the Text Walk work with multiple examples of long-worded questions in Mathematics? How could you guide students in this Text Walk?

VISUALISING

Reading in Role in Humanities (Legal Studies)

Reading in Role is a powerful dramatic activity that encourages students to empathise with the author of the text. It can be applied to nonfiction as well as fiction texts, and the Visualising activity can be used as a means of discussing the rationale behind laws and policies.

In this example, the School Strike 4 Climate article from The Conversation is used as stimulus material for the Reading in Role activity. Students are required to adopt a persona of a stakeholder in the climate issue, but also to reflect on existing laws and question why those laws might need to be changed from their role's point of view. Note how the original activity has been adjusted so that rather than students reading the original extract in role, they are *responding* to the article in role.

Example

Extract taken from www.theconversation.com/climate-change-will-cost-a-young-australian-up-to-245-000-over-their-lifetime-court-case-reveals-161175 (Phelan & Svenson, 2021)

> The Federal Court today dismissed a bid by a group of Australian teenagers seeking to prevent federal environment minister Sussan Ley from approving a coalmine extension in New South Wales.
>
> While the teens' request for an injunction was unsuccessful, a number of important developments emerged during the court proceedings. This included new figures on the financial costs of climate change to young Australians over their lifetimes.

An independent expert witness put the loss at between A$125,000 and A$245,000 per person. The calculation was a conservative one, and did not include health impacts, which were assessed separately.

The evidence was accepted by both the federal government's legal team and the judge. That it was uncontested represents an important shift. No longer are the financial impacts of climate change a vague future loss – they're now a tangible, quantifiable harm.

Read the complete article and adopt one of the following roles:

♦ A member of the group of teenagers who appealed to the court
♦ Minister Sussan Ley
♦ Dr Karl Mallon
♦ An Australian citizen aged between 17 and 25

Instructions

1. Read the article carefully and make notes on how you might perform this role. For example, how will you move? What will you say? Will you speak out loud their inner thoughts? Try to annotate the text with as much detail as possible to help your performance.
2. Write a short statement in response to the article from the perspective of your chosen role. The statement should last for one to three minutes.
3. After completing the Reading in Role activity, review the Proposed Climate Act at www.climateactnow.com.au/wp-content/uploads/2021/10/PMB_Ms-Steggall_Climate-Change-National-Framework-for-Adaptation-and-Mitigation-Bill-2021_151021.pdf
4. Write a response to the following prompt: **Political pressures such as student protests and coverage in the media can be effective in changing laws. Do you agree?**

Reflect

Dramatic performances can be unfamiliar territory, even for English teachers. There are many advantages, however, to having students perform. Stepping out of your comfort zone and incorporating dramatic activities like Reading in Role can enhance many areas of the curriculum.

- The final stage of the Reading in Role activity in the example is adapted from a senior secondary Legal Studies examination. What are the advantages of leading into the written response using the dramatic activity?
- How could you apply this activity to a practical subject, such as Design and Technology or Visual Arts?
- How could you use this activity in a subject like Health, for example, using UN Sustainability goals as a stimulus?

QUESTIONING

Four Questions in Visual Arts

Throughout the Visual Arts curriculum students are required to reflect on the styles of artists and the impact of various artistic movements. Students also need to adopt elements of certain styles and incorporate them into their own works. Questioning activities provide an excellent framework for students to think critically about other artists' works.

In this example of the Four Questions activity, students read an 'Explainer' article about cubism, focusing at the end on the work of Sonia Delaunay. They use the article and their other studies of cubism to form questions around the artist and the movement.

Example

Extract taken from Explainer: cubism www.theconversation.com/explainer-cubism-32553

There's more to cubism than Braque and Picasso

The canonised version of cubism placed a concern for the formal qualities of artwork over all other factors. This move, known as formalism, hermetically sealed off cubism from the complicated net of influences that had brought it into being.

Cinema, montage and French philosopher Henri Bergson's ideas on duration represented common points of influence in a wider desire to capture and understand time (the response of cubism would be seen as the capturing of an object from all of its possible perspectives).

Also, the politics of class and imperialism, and the pivotal role of women artists (marginalised later in a largely patriarchal discipline) are easily discovered in contemporary accounts of early avant-garde practice.

Sonia Delaunay, *Rythme,* 1938. Wikimedia Commons

Let's end, therefore, with this homage to Jewish-French-Russian artist Sonia Delaunay (1885–1979). I think of her as a kind of hinge holding together diverse avant-garde artists, poets and designers from across Europe.

She and her fellow artists developed a method of abstraction called 'orphism', sometimes called 'orphic cubism'. Named by her friend, the poet, critic and mouthpiece of cubism, Guillaume Apollinaire, orphism was an experiment with the simultaneous affect of colour and form to make a surface appear to vibrate.

Student questions written about the extract.

Question Type	Useful Verbs	Example Questions
Knowledge and comprehension	Tell List Describe Find State Name Explain	Who is Sonia Delaunay? What is 'orphism'?
Application	Show Illustrate Examine Solve	Examine Delaunay's Rythme and identify techniques the artist has used to make the work 'appear to vibrate'. Demonstrate your understanding of 'orphism' through the creation of an original piece.
Analysis	Analyse Compare Contrast Investigate Explore	Compare Delaunay's work to Picasso's cubism. Explore the use of colour in Delaunay's other pieces.
Synthesising and evaluating	Create Invent Construct Design Imagine Justify Argue Discuss	Design an artwork that blends elements of cubism and orphism to highlight the similarities and differences. The impact of formalism 'sealed off' cubism from the forces that created it. Discuss.

Reflect

Structuring questions in four different 'levels' highlights the difference between comprehension and analysis. As students grow in their reading skills, they should begin to move naturally between the different levels. Sometimes a simple comprehension question is just as important as a more complex synthesis question.

- Are the question levels tied to a particular age/ability, or should all students be attempting to move between the levels?
- How could this type of questioning be used to support another activity, such as the 'empathise' stage of a Design Thinking cycle in a Technology or STEM subject?
- How could these questions be used to develop 'examinable' responses at a senior level across different subject areas?

INFERRING

How do they feel? How do you know? in Health and Physical Education

The How do they feel? How do you know? inferring activity is an excellent way of encouraging students to both read between the lines of a text and to empathise with those involved. This makes it perfect for discussing complex issues such as those covered in Health and Physical Education, or any of the social sciences.

In this example, students read an article from the ABC on racism in sport, and are instructed to explore the article from a number of perspectives.

Example

Read the article 'Kids are being subjected to racist abuse at junior sports games. This club is taking a stand' at www.abc.net.au/news/2019-11-01/racism-in-junior-sport-australia-talks/11636174 (Kesteven, 2021)

Identify the main perspectives in the text, and then choose two to complete the How do they feel? How do you know? activity.

Perspective: Osman Jebara

How do they feel?	How do you know?	Quote/Paraphrase
Afraid, intimidated (aged 12)	☑ Actions ☑ Behaviour ☐ Interactions ☐ Dialogue ☐ Other	"I was just a kid... and I didn't want to say anything to him. So I just kept quiet and didn't look back at him."
Empowered, able to do something about racism	☐ Actions ☑ Behaviour ☐ Interactions ☐ Dialogue ☑ Other	Photograph of Jebara looking confident and powerful. "We need to educate these people."

Perspective: Derek Doffour

How do they feel?	How do you know?	Quote/Paraphrase
Angry	☑ Actions ☑ Behaviour ☐ Interactions ☐ Dialogue ☐ Other	"I went to confront him about it..."
Upset	☐ Actions ☐ Behaviour ☐ Interactions ☑ Dialogue ☐ Other	"It made me feel really upset because we just lost a game and I just got racially abused."

Reflect

This activity encourages students to look beyond the most obvious level of the text and to identify with the people involved. Consider how this could be applied to other nonfiction in other subject areas, particularly case studies in subjects that involved complex issues.

- Where could an activity like this lead? Think of how it could be used as a stimulus for a discussion or a longer activity such as a student-led case study.
- How could this activity be connected with others, such as the dramatic Reading in Role activity?
- How important is it that students are able to empathise with the subjects of articles and case studies like this?

SUMMARISING

Guided Summary in Humanities (History)

Many subjects include stimulus or other reading material, which can be fairly complex for students to decode. A Guided Summary provides extra structure around a text, reducing the literacy burden on the student. This example takes a document from Reconciliation Australia – itself a summary – and adds further support to the reading.

Example

Read the document *Five Fast Facts – NAIDOC Week* at www.reconciliation.org.au/wp-content/uploads/2021/10/Five-Fast-Facts-NAIDOC-Week.pdf and complete a Guided Summary along with the teacher.

Guided Summary

Step 1: Underline or highlight the parts of the text that contain the main ideas	
Step 2: Write out a list of the main ideas	1. NAIDOC week celebrates achievements and culture of Aboriginal and Torres Strait Islander People. 2. Started in 1938. 3. Celebrated by Aboriginal and Torres Strait Islander People. 4. NAIDOC week features an awards ceremony. 5. All Australians can participate in NAIDOC week.
Step 3: Combine any similar ideas together	1 and 4: NAIDOC week celebrates the achievements and culture of Aboriginal and Torres Strait Islander people, including an awards ceremony. 3 and 5: It is celebrated by Aboriginal and Torres Strait Islander people and can be celebrated by all Australians.
Step 4: Organise your list of ideas into order of importance, with the most important ideas at the top of the list	1 and 4: NAIDOC week celebrates the achievements and culture of Aboriginal and Torres Strait Islander people, including an awards ceremony. 2 Started in 1938. 3 and 5: It is celebrated by Aboriginal and Torres Strait Islander people and can be celebrated by all Australians.
Step 5: Write your summary as a paragraph. The paragraph should contain the most important information from the text	NAIDOC week celebrates the achievements and culture of Aboriginal and Torres Strait Islander people and includes an awards ceremony. It was started in 1938 and can be celebrated by Aboriginal and Torres Strait Islander people and all Australians.

Reflect

Summarising is an important but often overlooked skill. Students may default to copying notes or texts verbatim, which is not only time-consuming, but also requires very little processing of the information and therefore results in less comprehension and retention. This activity – like all of the Summarising and the later Synthesising activities – requires more conscious effort, but provides the reader with enough guidance and structure.

- What are the advantages of teaching summarising skills explicitly?
- Why is it useful to summarise even a short text like the one in the example?
- How could a guided summary be useful in other subject areas, such as with a practical report in Science, or a design brief in Technology?

SYNTHESISING

Text File in Product Design and Technology

The Text File is the ultimate Synthesising document. It is perfect for folio-based subjects, as it is designed to be flexible and frequently revisited and reviewed. In Product Design and Technology, the Text File can be built around a design thinking process, giving it an appropriate structure for the subject. In this case, the 'Text' is actually the initial design brief: a nonfiction text, which includes all of the initial information needed to meet the needs of the client or customer.

Example

Product Design and Technology Design Thinking Text File

This example demonstrates how a student might organise their Text File to match the stages of a Design Thinking Process. Each of the main headings would be followed by a subheading, and the information gathered over the course of the unit would eventually fill the Text File.

- **Empathise**
  - The design brief
  - Initial user surveys and market research
  - Information gathered about the problem
- **Define**
  - Synthesis of the 'empathise' stage
  - Brainstorms and planning
  - Definitions of the problem
- **Ideate**
  - SCAMPER document
  - Shared idea brainstorms
  - Idea selection
- **Prototype**
  - Digital prototype
  - Photos of paper prototype
  - Photos of rapid prototypes
- **Test**
  - User feedback
  - Survey results
  - Evaluation and discussion notes

Reflect

The Text File can be used for fiction and nonfiction texts, but it is designed to develop and grow over a longer period of time. This means that it must be constantly updated, and the teacher's role is to supervise the ongoing creation of the Text File and make sure it does not get left until the last minute.

- What are the advantages of treating the Design Brief as a 'text' and using it as the basis for a Text File, rather than creating a normal folio?
- What other texts in other subjects could form the basis of a Text File for development over a long period?
- What types of texts or studies are *not* suited to a text file?

Spreading the word

One of the most complex parts of integrating literacy practices into the whole-school curriculum is the competition for time. Some subjects have heavier content requirements than others, with curricula that feature much more explicit knowledge than the English curriculum. I often think that English teachers are lucky to have such an open and obviously skills-based curriculum; however, in Australia, the updated Australian Curriculum is seeing a shift away from content and towards skills in all subject areas, even those traditionally more content heavy, such as Science and The Humanities.

While we wait for the shift, the best way to encourage teachers to adopt these practices is through word of mouth. Work with teachers who are keen to try new techniques and to expand their understanding of literacy. When they are successful in improving the reading in their classrooms, make sure they are vocal about it. Look for opportunities to share ideas in faculty meetings or staff professional learning and try to get people on board organically.

All teachers have their own burdens, whether it is the volume of content they teach, issues with student engagement, behaviour or something else. Literacy teaching should not ever be just another burden – it should ultimately make our lives easier.

CHAPTER 12

CREATING A CULTURE OF READING

Most of this book has dealt with the *what* of reading, but it's important to step back and consider the *why*. There are countless studies into the various positive effects of reading, from the impact of reading on brain chemistry and neurological development (Stillman, 2021) to the effect of reading for pleasure on academic performance and vocabulary (Duff, Tomblin & Catts, 2015). There are also many proven links between reading and mental health, managing anxiety and improving overall wellbeing (Martinez, 2020).

Once we understand *why* reading is important, it's hard to argue against the benefits of creating a culture of reading in your school. Embedding the Reading Strategies into instruction is one way of doing this – making reading an interesting, engaging and student-centred experience will naturally build students' perceptions of reading. But the Reading Strategies are just one piece of a complex puzzle when it comes to building a culture of reading in a school.

This chapter explores a few ways to build on the Reading Strategies and create a culture of reading that extends beyond the classroom.

Develop a shared vision

First of all, it is important to develop a shared vision among the students and staff about what reading is, and why it is important. The introduction to this book explores some of that, but it is crucial that staff understand the complexities of reading as a process if they are to expect to improve reading among the students.

Starting with a small group of teachers – perhaps a subgroup of the English faculty – develop a vision for reading in the school. Gather data on current reading habits, for example, looking at library borrowing statistics, interviewing students and parents, or surveying cohorts of students to identify how frequently they read, and what they are reading. Once you have the information on current reading habits, ask yourselves 'why do we want to improve our reading culture?' This could be for any number of reasons. Perhaps you see reading as a way to improving academic results or performance. Perhaps you are interested in the links between reading and cognitive development or reading and wellbeing. Whatever your purpose, it should be unique to your school and your cohort of students.

Ask yourselves:

- How, when and what do our students currently read?
- Why do we want to improve the reading culture at our school?
- What outcomes would we expect to see if we improved the reading culture?
- Who are the key stakeholders in improving the culture? The teachers? The students? The parents? Library staff?
- What tactics and strategies will we use to improve the reading culture?
- What can we control? What is out of our control?
- How will we know that we have started to improve the reading culture?

Once you have answered some of these questions, consider how the vision for improving the reading culture sits in the 'bigger picture', for example, as part of the English faculty goals or the school strategic intent. The more comfortably the reading culture sits within the bigger systems of the school, the more likely it will be to stick.

Once you have a vision, investigate possibilities for improving the culture, such as those that follow.

Structured silent reading

Many schools have some form of silent reading built into their classes, particularly in Year 7-10 English classes. This might be 10 minutes of silent reading at the beginning or end of every lesson, or a block of time once a week. They may be tracked – ie with a reading log – or not. Whichever way you choose to organise a structured silent reading program, always refer back to the bigger picture of the reading culture vision.

Is it important that you track what the students are reading? If so, why? If not, what measures can you put in place to try to avoid students (and teachers!) taking liberties with the time? Silent reading can be an incredibly powerful way of giving students the time to read for pleasure, but it must be consistent and well managed.

Role modelling reading

Part of managing silent reading is the importance of modelling from the teacher. Students arrive at school with varying degrees of reading abilities and habits. Some have been read to from a young age, others not. Some will come from homes that have an abundance of books and reading materials, others not. A teacher is an important role model for students. During silent reading time, for example, the teacher should also be reading – not marking the roll, assessing work or other activities. The exception to this might be if you choose to have a form of conversation or reading log as part of the silent reading program. Even so, teachers should use any opportunities to model good reading habits, including talking about what they're currently reading and discussing books with students.

Classroom libraries

Classroom libraries are common in primary schools, but less so in secondary. This might be due to a lack of ownership of the classroom – it's often likely that one classroom might be home to multiple subjects and teachers. Or it might be a resourcing issue, particularly in larger schools. If possible, I'd recommend a box or a bookshelf per English class, particularly if the class is involved in a silent reading program. The books can be sourced from the school library if you're lucky enough to have one, or by donations. Try to create a classroom library that is diverse and has a variety of text types, forms and genres to engage as many students as possible. A classroom library also provides an extra resource for moments when students need something extra to do, or a little time and space to themselves.

Author engagement

Books aren't written in a bubble – they are living, breathing things that have been carefully crafted by an author. Sometimes, students find it hard to conceptualise the fact that books are crafted. You'll know that if you've ever written *too much description* or *retelling the story* on an essay – often, students fall back on recounting the events in texts as if they happened in real life, rather than commenting on the author's intent.

One way to improve this situation – and boost the profile of reading as a whole – is to regularly engage with authors. Some authors are incredibly amenable to school visits, offering a smorgasbord of workshops, talks and sometimes even fully developed song and dance performances. You'll find authors who are comfortable delivering stand-up comedy to a room full of Year 9s. Some authors might be a little quieter and more reserved, but perfectly suited to a sit-down Q&A session with senior students. The important thing for students to realise is that authors are *real people*. It escapes the attention of many students that writing is a profession, and that those who choose to do it have a particular skill set that they work at for a living.

Authors can range from very cheap to incredibly expensive, depending on their profile. If possible, I'd recommend at least one author visit per year level per year, spread out over the calendar. Preferably, some of these should be the authors of texts studied in class. If getting authors in is not a possibility, consider whether there are local literary festivals or events that could be used as an excursion.

Celebrating reading

There are many opportunities over the course of the year to celebrate reading. In Australia, events such Australia Reads, and the Australian Reading Hour occur regularly and are often well resourced. Promote them among the students *and* the staff. Book week is a staple of kindergartens and primary schools, but there's no reason it has to die out as soon as students reach Year 7.

If it's not feasible to send students to literary festivals, consider whether it is worth sending some of the staff. Again, refer back to the vision for improving reading culture in your school. Are the teachers part of it? Going to events such as the Melbourne Writers Festival can be a great opportunity for Professional Learning outside of the usual curriculum events. When those teachers return, their attitude towards reading (and writing) will hopefully be positive enough to drive some of your cultural shift.

Book clubs

Finally, book clubs are a long-standing favourite in terms of improving reading culture. Whether this means extracurricular book clubs for students – hosted by the school library perhaps – or book clubs for teachers, these communities offer an excellent way to boost the profile of reading.

Book clubs need time and organisation, and will require someone (or a team of someones) to make them sustainable. Thinking back to the vision, there may be a way to get additional buy-in from staff if a book club is strategically a part of something else. For example, a book club could be a great avenue into improving student voice or providing opportunities for Professional Learning among the staff.

CONCLUSION

We began with an attempt to define reading: what is reading, and how do we teach it? Through the six Strategies, we can view some of the complex processes involved in reading and target specific areas for students to work on, encouraging them to build their repertoire of skills and knowledge so that they can access increasingly complex texts.

One of the hardest parts of 'teaching reading' is the vast range of ability levels of our students – something that is often out of our control. So much of reading ability is based on experiences outside of the classroom, and every individual student (and teacher) has a different experience behind the eyes when confronted with a text. All we can do as teachers is continuously make the reading experience fun, engaging, challenging and relevant. Hopefully the activities in this book will help you to achieve that in your classroom.

What about writing?

Many of the activities in this book lead naturally to a written response. Hopefully the content of both the Strategies and part two of this book have made my position clear: start with reading. If students cannot read, understand and infer from texts, then at best they will only ever be able to parrot the teacher's writing. But once you have developed a strong culture of reading, and a curriculum that supports the complex skills involved in reading, it's time to grapple with the equally complex skills involved in writing.

Writing is a story for another time. We have developed a clear process for writing, which still leans heavily on close reading and the six Strategies, and uses modelling to guide students through exactly what is required from them, and how to get there. Our writing model, pictured below, will be the focus of another book: *Practical Writing Strategies*. But first, read!

Writing model

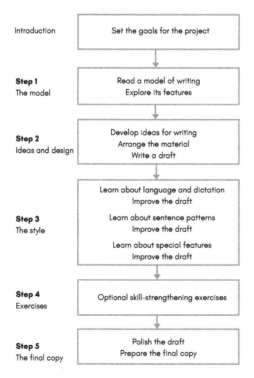

Introduction	Set the goals for the project
Step 1 The model	Read a model of writing Explore its features
Step 2 Ideas and design	Develop ideas for writing Arrange the material Write a draft
Step 3 The style	Learn about language and dictation Improve the draft Learn about sentence patterns Improve the draft Learn about special features Improve the draft
Step 4 Exercises	Optional skill-strengthening exercises
Step 5 The final copy	Polish the draft Prepare the final copy

REFERENCES

Andrejevic, M, Karim Obeid, A, Angus, D, & Burgess, J (2021). 'Facebook ads have enabled discrimination based on gender, race and age. We need to know how "dark ads" affect Australians'. Retrieved 6 December 2021, from www.theconversation.com/facebook-ads-have-enabled-discrimination-based-on-gender-race-and-age-we-need-to-know-how-dark-ads-affect-australians-168938

Bacalja, A, & Clark, K (2021). 'Playing with Digital Game Pedagogies', In Peterson, M, Yamazaki, K, & Thomas, M (Eds), *Digital games and language learning: Theory, Development and Implementation* (pp. 113-136). London, UK: Bloomsbury

Billman, A, & Pearson, PD (2013). Literacy in the disciplines. *Literacy Learning: The Middle Years*, 21(1)

Bloom, BS (1956). *Taxonomy of educational objectives: The Classification of Educational Goals*. New York: Longmans, Green

Boulet, M. (2021). 'Want to reduce your food waste at home? Here are the 6 best evidence-based ways to do it'. Retrieved 6 December 2021, from https://theconversation.com/want-to-reduce-your-food-waste-at-home-here-are-the-6-best-evidence-based-ways-to-do-it-168561

Bowler, J (2021). 'The Sensitivity of Human Fingertips Is Greater Than We Ever Imagined'. Retrieved 6 December 2021, from www.sciencealert.com/our-fingertips-have-a-secret-weapon-that-makes-them-remarkably-sensitive-to-touch

Bryant, J (2021). 'Explainer: cubism'. Retrieved 6 December 2021, from www.theconversation.com/explainer-cubism-32553

Bui, NT, Kang, H, & Urban, J (2021). 'Heavy metal pollution: How can we make water safe to drink?' *Science Journal for Kids and Teens.* Retrieved 6 December 2021, from www.sciencejournalforkids.org/articles/heavy-metal-pollution-how-can-we-make-water-safe-to-drink

Clemens, A (2021). 'When the Mind's Eye Is Blind'. Retrieved 6 December 2021, from www.scientificamerican.com/article/when-the-minds-eye-is-blind1

Dalton, J, & Smith, D (1986) *Extending Children's Special Abilities – Strategies for primary classrooms.* Melbourne: Curriculum Branch, Schools Division

Derewianka, B, & Jones, P (2016). *Teaching Language in Context.* Melbourne: Oxford University Press Australia & New Zealand

Duff, D, Tomblin, JB, & Catts, H (2015). The Influence of Reading on Vocabulary Growth: A Case for a Matthew Effect. *Journal of speech, language, and hearing research: JSLHR*, 58(3), 853–864. www.doi.org/10.1044/2015_JSLHR-L-13-0310

Filiatrault-Veilleux, P, Bouchard, C, Trudeau, N, & Desmarais, C (2015). Inferential comprehension of 3-6 year olds within the context of story grammar: a scoping review. *International Journal of Language & Communication Disorders,* 50(6), 737-749. www.doi.org/10.1111/1460-6984.12175

Gee, JP (2004). *Situated language and learning: A critique of traditional schooling.* London: Routledge

Gilbert, J, Reiner, M, & Nakhleh, M (2008). *Visualization.* Dordrecht: Springer

Hamer, A (2021). 'Here's Why Smells Trigger Such Vivid Memories'. Retrieved 6 December 2021, from www.discovery.com/science/Why-Smells-Trigger-Such-Vivid-Memories

Hochman, J, Wexler, N, & Lemov, D (2017). *The Writing Revolution: A Guide to Advancing Thinking Through Writing in All Subjects and Grades.* Hoboken: Jossey-Bass

Keene, E, & Zimmermann, S (1997). *Mosaic of thought.* Portsmouth, NH: Heinemann

Kesteven, S (2021). 'Kids are being subjected to racist abuse at junior sports games. This club is taking a stand'. Retrieved 18 November 2021, from www.abc.net.au/news/2019-11-01/racism-in-junior-sport-australia-talks/11636174

Khazan, O (2021). 'The Myth of "Learning Styles"'. Retrieved 6 December 2021, from www.theatlantic.com/science/archive/2018/04/the-myth-of-learning-styles/557687

Martinez, K (2020). 'Reading Books Can Benefit Your Mental Health'. www.stepupformentalhealth.org/reading-books-can-benefit-hour-mental-health

Morrison, K, Ritchhart, R, & Church, M (2013). *Making Thinking Visible.* San Francisco, California: Jossey-Bass

Phelan, L, & Svenson, J (2021). 'Climate change will cost a young Australian up to $245,000 over their lifetime, court case reveals'. Retrieved 6 December 2021, from www.theconversation.com/climate-change-will-cost-a-young-australian-up-to-245-000-over-their-lifetime-court-case-reveals-161175

Rayner, K, & Reichle, ED (2010). Models of the reading process. *Wiley interdisciplinary reviews. Cognitive science,* 1(6), 787–799. www.doi.org/10.1002/wcs.68

Reconcilliation.org (2021). 'Five Fast Facts – NAIDOC Week'. Retrieved 6 December 2021, from www.reconciliation.org.au/wp-content/uploads/2021/10/Five-Fast-Facts-NAIDOC-Week.pdf

Scholastic Corporation. *Barriers to Equity in Education.* Retrieved from scholastic.com: www.scholastic.com/site/teacher-principal-school-report/key-findings/equity-in-education.html

Stillman, J (2021). 'This Is How Reading Rewires Your Brain, According to Neuroscience'. Retrieved 6 December 2021, from www.inc.com/jessica-stillman/reading-books-brain-chemistry.html

Quak, M, London, RE, & Talsma, D (2015). 'A multisensory perspective of working memory'. *Frontiers in human neuroscience,* 9, 197. www.doi.org/10.3389/fnhum.2015.00197

Tllos, A, & Woolley, J (2009). The development of children's ability to use evidence to infer reality status. *Child Development,* 80(1), 101–114. www.doi.org/10.1111/j.1467-8624.2008.01248.x

APPENDIX

Templates within this appendix are also available to download from https://leonfurze.com/prs/

Appendix 1
Chapter 2: Visualising – Activity 1: Sensory Scenes

Sensory Scenes	
Name: Text/extract:	
Sounds: Describe the sounds	Smells: Describe the smells
Sight: Draw a picture of the scene	
Taste: Describe the taste	Textures: Describe the textures or attach a material

Appendix 2

Chapter 3: Questioning – Activity 2: Why? Why? Why?

Why? Why? Why?	
Statement (by teacher)	
First 'Why...?'	
First answer	
Second 'Why...?'	
Second answer	
Third 'Why...?'	
Third answer	

Summary sentence

_____

_____

_____

Appendix 3

Chapter 3: Questioning – Activity 3: Text Interrogation

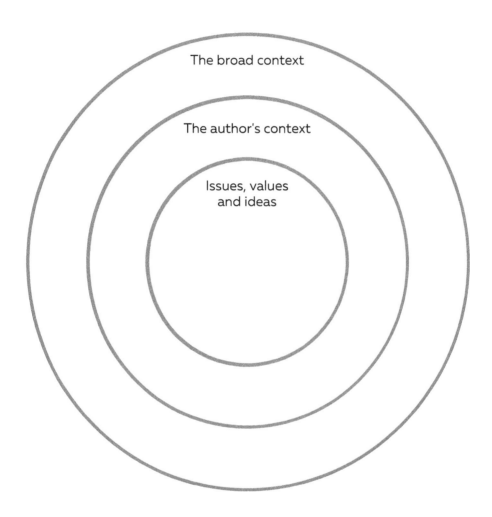

The broad context

The author's context

Issues, values
and ideas

Appendix 4

Chapter 5: Summarising – Activity 1: Guided Summary

Guided Summary	
Step 1: Underline or highlight the parts of the text that contain the main ideas	
Step 2: Write out a list of the main ideas	
Step 3: Combine any similar ideas together	
Step 4: Organise your list of ideas into order of importance, with the most important ideas at the top of the list	
Step 5: Write your summary as a paragraph. The paragraph should contain the most important information from the text	

Appendix 5

Chapter 6: Synthesising – Activity 2: Strategy Hub

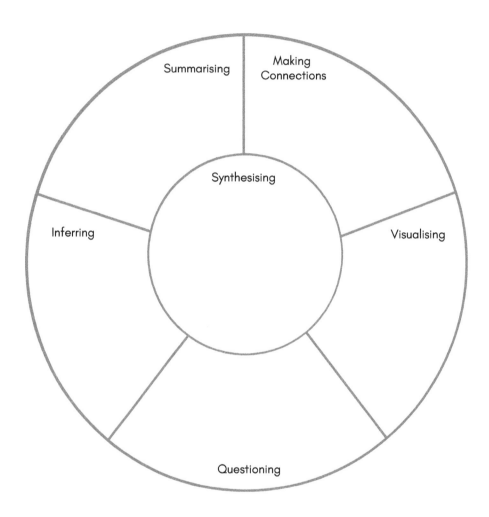

Lightning Source UK Ltd.
Milton Keynes UK
UKHW010622111122
411892UK00022B/373